THE GOOD COOK'S BOOK OF

Oil & Vinegar

THE GOOD COOK'S BOOK OF
Oil & Vinegar

WITH MORE THAN 100 RECIPES

Michele Anna Jordan

Foreword by M. F. K. Fisher
Illustrations by Michel Stong

ADDISON-WESLEY PUBLISHING COMPANY
Reading, Massachusetts   Menlo Park, California   New York
Don Mills, Ontario   Wokingham, England   Amsterdam   Bonn
Sydney   Singapore   Tokyo   Madrid   San Juan
Paris   Seoul   Milan   Mexico City   Taipei

Many of the designations used by manufacturers and sellers to distinguish their products are claimed as trademarks. Where those designations appear in this book and Addison-Wesley was aware of a trademark claim, the designations have been printed in initial capital letters.

Library of Congress Cataloging-in-Publication Data

Jordan, Michele Anna.
The good cook's book of oil & vinegar / Michele Anna Jordan;
foreword by M. F. K. Fisher; illustrations by Michel Stong.
p.   cm.

Includes bibliographical references and index.
ISBN 0-201-57075-0
1. Cookery (Vinegar)   2. Oils and fats.   I. Title.   II. Title:
Oil & Vinegar.
TX819.V5J67 1992
641.6'385—dc20   92-8278
CIP

Cover and interior illustrations by Michel Stong
Cover design by Diana Coe
Text design by Karen Savary
Set in 11-point Weiss by Carol Woolverton

4 5 6 7 8 9 10-DOH-9998979695
Fourth printing, January 1995

For Gina Renée, my firstborn,
and
Nicolle Michele, my last,
with love

CONTENTS

RECIPES BY COURSE

FOREWORD

Comparisons are said to be odious, but I would not find it odious at all to have anything that I have written about either oil or vinegar compared with this book. In other words, Michele Jordan and I seem to agree and I am proud to admit it.

Of course, I don't recognize many of the private product names given and I admit to real ignorance about the uses of fruit or berry vinegars. I do know and love anything connected with *aceto balsamico*, which for some reason I have never thought of as being especially exotic.

I also confess to a complete ignorance of using pure virgin olive oil for anything except lubricating the umbilical cords of new babies, until I was perhaps in my early teens and my mother had finally stopped reproducing. It was about then that my grandmother Holbrook died too, and the scrubby little two-ounce bottle of olive oil, which had stayed on a shelf in the medicine cabinet, was correctly moved to a shelf in the kitchen cooler. It automatically became a quart bottle or a two-quart tin. In other words, I am an addict but not a snob.

I am very glad to be in the good company of Michele

Jordan. I suppose we are both more addicts than snobs, but neither of us cares one whit. I think Michele uses both oil and vinegar more in cooking than I do, but that's all right too since we both know what oil and vinegar are for: They are as necessary to us as water, or almost. And that is as it should be.

M. F. K. FISHER
GLEN ELLEN, 1991

ACKNOWLEDGMENTS

My two daughters, Gina Renée and Nicolle Michele, were the vinaigrette of my salad days, and together they inspire, in a deep and essential way, all that I do. This book has been written for them, with tremendous love.

In addition, I thank everyone who tasted new recipes, especially Jerry Hertz who braved through the vinegar sorbet that he still talks about, read rough drafts, accepted swigs of olive oil, and generally put up with me. Many people eased the way and here I especially acknowledge M. F. K. Fisher, with great affection; David Browne, again and always, with gratitude; John Boland and James Carroll, my publisher and my editor at *The Paper* and two of the most wonderful people on the planet; Anna Cherney, for her friendship and inspiration; Elizabeth Carduff, for her warmth and invaluable guidance; my editor, John Harris, for being himself; Madeleine Kamman, for the essential fine-tuning and the girl talk; Ginny Stanford, for her enduring friendship and support; Greil Marcus, for his encouragement, for his exuberant praise of my cooking, and for his wonderful books, which provide the best escape imaginable from things culinary; everyone who so enthusiastically supported my first book; and especially Jan Costello, J. J. Wilson, Lou Preston, Jennifer Bice, Stephen Schack, Nancy Dobbs, John Kramer, Dane Osborn, Perry Jasper, and Nick Topolos.

A number of people contributed technical advice and helped me fine-tune the manuscript, and I thank them profusely for their contributions: the elegant and articulate Darrell Corti of Corti Brothers; the delightful Dante Bagnani; L. J. Diggs, the Vinegar Man; Dr. George York and Dr. Bruce German of the University of California at Davis; Liesel Hofmann; and the charmingly meticulous Frances Bowles, who catches all of my mistakes.

And finally, I give my overwhelming gratitude, praise, and admiration to the incomparable Michel Stong, who made my image of the book come alive with her beautiful art.

INTRODUCTION

"Oil and vinegar?" said a friend who is a musician. "Is that a book about men and women?" I was astonished at this, probably the most interesting comment I heard when mentioning this book, but conceded that I could see her point. Opposites in nearly every way, oil and vinegar in one form or another have been companions since the beginning of our own history, a culinary parallel to that most pervasive of all unions of opposites, male and female. It was not a comparison that had ever occurred to me, though, and I still laugh when I remember the sincerity and assuredness that accompanied her statement. But who is the vinegar, I wondered; who, the oil? Regardless, look at this book as a celebration of their marriage.

The need for a cookbook like this one becomes apparent every time I mention the topic. Except for the single exception above, people respond, "Oh, yes, a book on salad dressings." That these wonderful and varied ingredients, a panorama of flavors and textures and aromas, are viewed in most people's minds nearly exclusively as components of salad dressings is revealing. Chefs rely on the qualities and nuances of vinegars and oils to inform diverse cuisines, and yet there is a void in our culinary literature. The topic is not widely addressed. Certainly, salad dressings are one of the important and delicious results of mixing together an oil and a vinegar. These mixtures add spark not only to salads, but also to seafoods, meats, vegetables, pastas, and grains. There are other mixtures that are equally delicious and important, marinades, for example, and emulsified sauces such as mayonnaises and *aïolis*. As I have researched the topic, developed many recipes, and discovered others, I have realized just how diverse and delicious a subject this is.

Both oil and vinegar are simple, essential foods that have been with us for thousands of years, ingredients many of us see and use and eat daily, that appear in a multitude of recipes in all cuisines the world around. There are technical journals that speak to the scientific and medical communi-

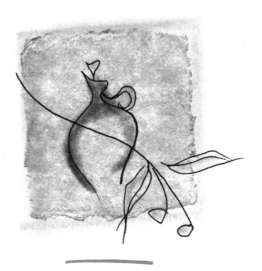

ties, and there are slim pamphlets put out by producers of various oils and vinegars. There are a few small booklets that contain a great deal of misinformation about vinegar. A slim volume, *Oil, Vinegar, and Seasonings*, appeared in early 1991 but again, with limited scope. Olive oil stands alone in its legacy of literary inspiration; there are three substantial works on the topic, including *The Feast of the Olive* by Maggie Klein, a lovely, informative book that has influenced me greatly. I found no basic text that covered the broader subject of oils or vinegars in general, no cookbook that treated the ingredients comprehensively. I have attempted to make a start, offering here, not only what I view as the essential information, the tools for navigating the vast pantry of oils and vinegars now readily available to the domestic cook, but also many of my favorite recipes, dishes that would either not exist or be drastically different were it not for a special quality contributed by a favorite vinegar or a distinctive oil.

It is not possible to discuss specific foods without addressing the issue of personal biases. This book reflects mine in many ways. First and last, I write about the things I love, in this case the olive oils and the vinegars that do the right thing when they cross my lips. Yes, I am an addict when it comes to things culinary and I think that is as it should be. We have to eat, and I believe we might as well make it as much a thrill as possible. I love a good olive oil so much that I am not averse to taking a healthy swig directly from the bottle. It is this enthusiasm—obsession, if you prefer—that shapes my approach.

Now, I do not expect everyone to respond as I do and you should keep my personal preferences in mind. When I tell you about my favorite olive oil or talk about my reasons for liking toasted sesame oil, I am in part revealing a purely subjective reaction. For flavor, I most often prefer unrefined olive oils from the heart of Tuscany, "big" oils with lots of peppery fire slipping down the back of my throat. When I can find it, I relish the intensity of the extra virgin olive from Poggio Lamentano, the only olive oil I have come across that dates its production. Ardoino offers several wonderful olive oils from the Italian Riviera, and I'm especially fond of the Biancardo, a late-harvest, light golden oil, that is both intense and delicate, delicious drizzled on poached seafood or a baked potato. It is not made every year, but only when weather conditions have been such to allow it. I have had exquisite oils from Antinori, though I have also tasted oils of that brand that I have not cared for. When I must use an oil from a major producer, I favor Sasso or Monini extra virgin olive oils, which have a consistently pleasant taste at a reasonable price. Sasso or Ardoino pure olive oil is well suited to high-temperature cooking, when the flavors of more delicate oils would be ruined. I find the other major brands unacceptable. Although I feel disloyal saying so, I prefer European olive oils to those produced in California. Very good oils are produced from the olive groves of California, but not great oils. Nick Sciabica & Sons, in the Central Valley, produces consistently high-quality California olive oils, and their Sevillano Fall Harvest is lovely, but even at their best they do not compare with the finest Italian and French oils. As better and better oils begin to arrive from Spain, we will be offered a larger range of high-quality oils. My recent discovery of Spectrum Naturals' unrefined corn oil was an exhilarating surprise:

corn oil so full of the flavor of real corn! The increased availability of unrefined oils that retain their natural aromas and flavors is great news for cooks.

I take a more subtle approach to my vinegars, preferring an acidity level no higher than 6 percent, or 6.5 percent if it is a particularly rich vinegar. I like a red wine vinegar in which the character of the wine still shines through, and prefer the clear, light champagne vinegar to other white wine vinegars. With berry vinegars, the richer the better, and again, that frequently implies low acid. Kozlowski Farms berry vinegars, made near my home in Sonoma County, have only 4.5 percent acidity and allow the rich flavor of the berries to dominate. I find balsamic vinegar delightful, use it frequently, and hope someday to possess a little of the true *aceto balsamico tradizionale*, whose story I find so intriguing. Personal preferences do not, however, make it impossible to judge objectively. There are standards of quality, absolutes of freshness, and standards of production and storage that we can all use to ferret out our favorites in a vast and confusing marketplace. One can distinguish the quality of a food or a particular product while not necessarily favoring it for personal use. Thus, I present to you here, not only my own favorites, but also what I hope will be guidelines for finding your own.

PART ONE

All About Oils

WHAT IS OIL?

What, exactly, is an oil? The answer is simple: Oil is a fat. The only distinction that places oil in its own category is its melting point. In both common and scientific usage, fats that are solid at room temperature are considered fats; those that are liquid at room temperature, oils. This distinction generally follows the divisions into animal and vegetable as well. Animal fats, such as butter, lard, beef suet, and duck fat, remain firm at room temperature; most of the familiar vegetable fats—olive oil, corn oil, safflower oil, nut oils—are usually easily poured. The vegetable fats that remain almost solid, even at room temperature, are palm, coconut, and *dendê* oils. They have some of the highest saturated ratios of all fats (see the chart on page 5) and are thus of negligible nutritional value.

In cooking, a fat has two primary purposes, to lubricate and to transfer heat. Some specialty oils, notably olive oil and several of the nut oils, are used for the flavor they impart. With so many oils available on the market these days and with such a wide variety of nutritional and culinary claims made for them, it is important to develop a basic understanding of what is being offered.

Fats and oils, members of a group of biological compounds called lipids, are triglycerides. They are composed primarily of glycerol and three long hydrocarbon chains called fatty acids. Detailed knowledge of the chemistry of fat is not essential to an understanding of its nutritional and culinary properties, but is helpful when you want to understand its effects in the kitchen and in the body.

The primary function of fat in the diet is the storage of energy. Fats contain more than twice as much energy as do carbohydrates and thus are an efficient way for an animal to carry a source of extra fuel. In addition, fats provide the pleasant rich taste of many foods and give us the sensation of being full, thus delaying the recurrence of hunger. The body assimilates fat more slowly than it assimilates other nutrients and this accounts for the feeling of satisfaction.

It is important to address the misconception that fats are completely superfluous to our nutrition. A belief popular these days is that, if we were being nutritionally correct, we would eliminate all fats from our diet and, lacking in willpower, we must struggle at all times to avoid the attractive culinary bad boy as much as possible. This is simply untrue. One of the reasons fats taste so good is that they are essential to our physical health and well-being. It was once difficult to assure we had enough fat in our diets, and thus it was essential to our survival and evolution as a species to want them, to seek them out because they pleased us. We have come a long way since our ancestors hunted for their food, gathering what was at hand and, if they were lucky, finding enough dietary fat to supply their needs. Several developments have led to our being faced today with the need to reduce the fat we ingest, even while we are still motivated by what was once a key to our survival: the craving for their rich taste. Certain fats are still essential; others, especially in significant amounts, may be detrimental to our health. With the increased availability and marketing of prepared foods, there is a substantial amount of hidden fat in the average person's diet. Fortunately, we can use fats in our diet while cutting back on quantity and on those that might harm us.

STORING OILS *All oils, and especially virgin olive oils and other unrefined oils, are best kept away from heat and light. A cool, dark cupboard is the best environment for oils when they are not sitting on your work counter. Tinted glass, porcelain, or stainless steel are the best materials for containers; oils should never be stored in plastic or in reactive metals. Certain oils—walnut and hazelnut oils, for example—are very unstable and should be refrigerated.*

The words polyunsaturated, monounsaturated, and saturated scream at us from marketing claims, product labels, nutritional charts, guidelines, and warnings, but what do the terms actually mean? The question of saturation has to do with the structure of the molecule of the fatty acid in question. The molecules of saturated fats are filled to capacity—that is, saturated—with hydrogen atoms. These fats are stable and align themselves into more densely packed solids than do their unsaturated cousins; thus we find that fats that consist of a high percentage of saturated fatty acids are solid at room temperature. In the molecular chain of an unsaturated fat is a double carbon bond that is capable of uniting with other molecules, creating an instability so that these fats are less stable, liquid, and more subject to oxidation and the resulting breakdown in flavor that we call rancidity. Fats with just one double carbon bond are known as mono-unsaturates; those with more than one are known as poly-unsaturates.

For culinary and nutritional purposes, it is important to understand the sources of the fats we eat and whether they are saturated or unsaturated. Substantial research has indicated that saturated fats pose the greatest threat to health, particularly in their tendency to raise levels of blood cholesterol and contribute to such diseases as arteriosclerosis, or hardening of the arteries.

Fats come from animal and vegetable sources. Animal fats contain cholesterol, are about 50 percent saturated and

50 percent unsaturated, and are not the focus of this book. We need only understand the distinction between animal fats and vegetable fats. Vegetable fats come from a variety of raw materials and are, in general, higher in unsaturates than are animal fats. They are the focus of our attention. It is essential to stress that no vegetable fats contain

FATTY ACID PROFILE OF COMMON CULINARY OILS
(PERCENTAGES OR PARTS PER 100)

TYPE OF OIL	SATURATED FATTY ACIDS	MONO- UNSATURATED FATTY ACIDS	POLY- UNSATURATED FATTY ACIDS
ALMOND	9	65	26
AVOCADO	20	70	10
CANOLA (Rapeseed)	6	60	34
COCONUT	90	7.5	2.5
CORN	13	27	60
COTTONSEED	24	26	50
GRAPESEED	12	17	71
HAZELNUT	10	76	14
MUSTARD	1	76	23
OLIVE	10	82	8
PEANUT	17	61	22
PUMPKIN SEED	9	34	57
RICE BRAN	19	42	39
SAFFLOWER	6.6	16.4	77
SESAME	14	40	46
SOYBEAN	14	24	62
SUNFLOWER	13	21	66
WALNUT	16	28	54

Sources: *Foods & Nutrition Encyclopedia*, 1983; *Composition of Foods*, 1963; *The Lipid Handbook*, 1986; *Spectrum Naturals Kitchen Guide*, 1990.

cholesterol. With a few negligible exceptions, cholesterol is present only in animals. There are, however, saturated fatty acids in vegetable fats, which can contribute to the increased production of cholesterol in the body, though the percentage is nearly always considerably lower than that in animal fats. Vegetable oils are extracted from their source material—nuts, seeds, grains, and fruits—by a variety of processes ranging from simple to complex. Some commercial oils are blends of two or more extracted plant oils. None of them contains cholesterol.

WHAT IS MARGARINE? Ostensibly a substitute for butter, margarine is made of vegetable oil that has been artificially saturated through a process of hydrogenation to make it more stable at room temperature. The process is similar to the method used for making plastics. Tub margarine contains about 13 percent saturated fat; cube margarine contains about 20 percent. A French invention of the early 1800s, margarine was being produced in quantities in this country by 1880. There was great resistance to its general use, especially by the dairy industry, and it was not until 1950 that government restrictions and heavy taxes were lifted. Until 1967, it was illegal in Wisconsin to sell margarine that had been dyed yellow.

If you wish to avoid the artificially saturated, refined oils used in margarine, a good substitute is a blend of equal parts of butter and an unrefined vegetable oil. Bring the butter to room temperature and blend it with an equal quantity of oil. For flavor as well as nutritional value, I recommend olive oil.

Reliable studies continue to indicate that mono-unsaturated oils are the healthiest. They reduce the level of "bad" cholesterol (LDL) in our systems without reducing the "good" cholesterol (HDL) (see page 8). Polyunsaturated oils reduce the level of both types of cholesterol. Saturated fats can contribute to increased levels of blood serum cholesterol and, if their source is animal products, they themselves contain cholesterol.

FATS AND HEALTH

Very little is known about the health effects of transforming millions of confident, healthy people into cholesterol neurotics. And there is even evidence to suggest that stress and worry about anything—including fats in the diet—can itself raise blood cholesterol levels.

Robert Ornstein and David Sobel,
Healthy Pleasures, Addison-Wesley, 1989

Over the past several years, fat and cholesterol have been the subjects of a multitude of studies. The primary concern has been how and to what extent certain types of fats and blood cholesterol levels increase or decrease our chances of developing heart disease, although the effect of fats on the development of certain types of cancers has also been addressed.

Cholesterol is essential to a variety of bodily functions, including the production of cell membranes, hormones, and bile acids. Without it, we would die. Many factors determine the cholesterol level of a particular individual, including uncontrollable variables such as age and heredity. Smoking, stress, level of physical activity, weight, and diet are the factors that we can influence. There are two types of cholesterol, low-density lipoproteins (LDL, the "bad" cholesterol) and high-density lipoproteins (HDL, the "good" cholesterol). Simply put, LDL is responsible for the buildup of plaque in the arteries, which in turn leads to arteriosclerosis. Numerous factors influence this buildup and only some of them are understood.

Aspects of cholesterol studies have been inaccurately heralded in the press, and reported in simplified ways that obscure the true results. Consequently, we are becoming a society with a raging fear of fat, a fear that may itself contribute to ill health as much as or more than does the feared substance. There is an aspect of truth in the claim that dietary fats increase blood cholesterol levels; there is no evidence to support the length to which the issue has been taken by dietary extremists, that all dietary fat must be eliminated.

There are several explanations for this current hysteria about fat. The demands of journalism, of daily news stories, often result in information simplified to the point that it cannot present an accurate picture of the subject. Just a short time ago, we were warned against fats of any kind. Currently, we are told that omega-3, -6, and -9 fatty acids are not only healthy but also essential and that we should seek them in oil—that is, fat—supplements. The most accurate conclusion one comes to after looking more closely at the research is that we are a long way from resolving the issue.

Another factor at work in the controversy about fat is the strong bias against pleasure that runs through American culture. The reasons for this proscription are best addressed elsewhere, but it influences significantly the way in which Americans think about food. Studies have shown that periodic indulgence in a fat-rich, thoroughly enjoyed meal does absolutely nothing to raise the cholesterol level of those who in general must restrict their diets. The pleasure derived from such a meal may be highly beneficial to our general well-being. Of course, I am not recommending that those with medical problems should be guided by pleasure alone. I am, however, cautioning against embracing cure-all fads or resorting to culinary extremism.

THE MARKETING AND MISMARKETING OF OILS

Does an oil have any nutritional value? How does it differ from a fat? Does it contain cholesterol? Are some oils healthier than others? How are oils produced? Replies—accurate and inaccurate, honest and intentionally deceptive—shout at us from product labels and market shelves, but few really offer the information that is essential if we are to make informed choices. That is not, after all, the function of advertising. It is up to the consumer, up to you, to learn what you need to know to make intelligent choices about the oils you use. Navigating the marketplace is really not difficult at all, once you've acquired a certain, basic knowledge. The Food and Drug Administration is revising labeling restrictions and requirements that will correct some of the confusion and prohibit many of the misleading claims currently on product labels.

Advertising quickly exploits scientific claims about our diets, and because of the attention on fats, it is these products that are being victimized by marketers. Various studies about good fats and bad fats have spawned numerous claims in the marketplace about which oils are best. Some are outright claims to lower cholesterol; many are simply statements of the lack of the substance in a given product.

There is an element of accuracy in some claims, but marketers have moved the issue toward the ridiculous with labeling that plays on people's fear, ignorance, and vulnerability. "Contains no salt!" a label for rice bran oil may shout; "Olive Oil Lite!" screams another; "No cholesterol" beckons yet another. Such labels reveal a cycle of exploitation, a vulnerability in the consumer that marketers readily manipulate. One reads these days that salt, for example, may not be healthy and then, seeing an oil carrying the legend, "No Salt," chooses that one over the others on the shelf, even at a higher price. The advertiser's claim is unconscionable because pure oil never contains salt.

Similarly, the product labeled Olive Oil Lite contains exactly the same number of calories, about 125 per tablespoon, as any other oil, but the American public has been conditioned to associate the coined word "lite" with fewer calories, so again, people choose the product, unaware that they are being manipulated. Olive Oil Lite is simply olive oil refined to remove its characteristic flavor and color.

There is no cholesterol in vegetable oils and never has been. But when a shiny new label proclaims its absence, the consumer reaches toward it. Such labeling claims as these cause confusion, and their lack of accurate information will only increase the consumers' cynicism.

What should one look for on an oil label? First of all, if you have any doubts about what may be in the oil, check the ingredients list, required of all packaged and bottled products. The label must list everything that is in the oil. Certain oils, especially "Wok Oil" and some sesame oils, contain flavorings, components that are best added fresh by the cook at the time of preparation. Some otherwise blameless oils are mixed with cottonseed oil or soybean oil, neither of which is a good choice for cooking, regardless of your specific needs (see page 37). Look for method of extraction, and whether the oil is refined or unrefined. The country of production will often be listed on labels, but can be misleading. "Product of Italy," for example, means only that the raw material, the oil, was *processed* in Italy. The oil itself may have been imported from Greece or Spain. A notation that an oil has been estate grown and bottled indicates that the oil has been produced in a specific place and not imported from elsewhere and then bottled. Without that notation, chances are that oils sold under small, specialty labels were grown and produced elsewhere.

THE MANUFACTURE OF VEGETABLE OILS

The process of making oil is a process of extraction, a means of releasing the fatty juices of grains, seeds, nuts, and fruits. There are many ways to do it, and the ancient method of mechanical extraction, without the use of chemical solvents, is still used to produce the highest-quality oils. Oil can be divided into two categories, unrefined and refined. Unrefined oils provide the highest overall quality and the fullest, most complex taste, but both have their place in our pantries.

UNREFINED OILS

The function of unrefined processing is to expel the oil from its raw material by mechanical means and with minimal heat. "Cold-pressed," a term once common on oil labels, is misleading. The only oil that is actually pressed cold is olive oil and then only by the smaller producers. Other sources of oils—nuts, seeds, and grains—are cleaned mechanically and then heated. The oil may be warmed, frequently as high as 160 degrees F., and then pressed out mechanically. It can be labeled "100 percent expeller pressed." Olive oil, once the pulp has been crushed and the oil pressed out, may be centrifuged to separate the oil from the other juices. Virgin olive oil is by definition unrefined.

Unrefined oils have a richer appearance than their pale, refined cousins, as well as more flavor and aroma. They also contain essential nutrients and vitamins that are removed in refining. Until recently, olive oil was the only unrefined oil that had any currency in the culinary world. Other oils—corn, walnut, hazelnut, and peanut come to mind—that retain a surprising amount of rich flavor when unrefined are creating many new culinary possibilities. Unrefined oils are perfect for finishing a dish. A splash of toasted sesame oil, extra virgin olive oil, or unrefined walnut oil will add a pleasing, rounded depth of flavor to many recipes. It is important to keep in mind that unrefined oils have a lower smoke point than refined oils. Because of this, and because their delicate flavors break down at elevated temperatures, you should not use unrefined oils for deep-frying or other cooking that requires high heat. They should be stored away from heat and light as well.

REFINED OILS

Most oils on the market today are chemically extracted by a process that uses solvents made from petroleum. The raw material is cleaned and crushed and a solvent is applied to draw out the oil. Once the solvent has extracted the oil from the raw material, the fluid is boiled to remove the solvent. The oil then must be refined. Most expeller-pressed oils are also later refined. Oils produced by both methods of extraction—expeller and solvent—are subjected to identical methods of refining. The label is not required to identify the type of extraction process.

The process of refining strips an oil of its color, its scent, and according to many experts, its nutrients. A process called degumming removes the lecithin, chlorophyll, vitamin E, and all minerals present in the oil. The addition of an alkaline solution removes any other substances that linger through the first step of refining. Diatomaceous earth is added to bleach the oil, and then the oil is steamed to deodorize it. Finally, the oil goes through a process called winterizing: It is cooled and filtered to remove any constituent that may cause cloudiness at lower temperatures. Refined oils do have their place in the culinary world. For high-temperature cooking—deep-frying, for example—refined oils are perfect. Certain recipes demand an oil be as flavor-less as possible. It should be kept in mind, however, that their functions, just like their flavors, their nutritional value, and their scents, are limited.

Americans are accustomed to refined oils that are not cloudy and that have little or no scent, in large part because they have been the most readily available. Although the heartier and full-flavored extra virgin olive oils are becoming increasingly popular, there is still a great deal of resistance to highly flavored oils and to cloudy, unfiltered oils. With their increasing availability, however, the particular culinary properties of unrefined oils should become more apparent, and the possibilities of home cooking expand to include their contribution.

VEGETABLE SEED OILS

Many plants have seeds rich with oil, but only some actually yield an edible oil. Many of our most common vegetable oils have been with us for centuries. In ancient times, oils were drawn from what was at hand. In Greece, olive oil, walnut oil, and oil from the opium poppy were used. In Africa and Mesopotamia, olive oil and sesame oil were used and in Egypt, linseed oil (from flax) and radish seed oil. Asian oils included soybean and coconut palm and in the Americas groundnut, corn, and sunflower seed oil were used. Many of these seed oils used in the ancient world have disappeared as we have found better sources. Some remain, as essential to our cuisine now as they were so long ago.

Sesame seeds probably provided the world's first

source of oil, because olives have particular requirements that limit the regions where they thrive. Sesame, with its particularly short growth cycle, can thrive almost anywhere. The seeds themselves are rather oily, and it would not have taken early societies—restricted to a simple process of expelling oil by mechanical means—long to discover that their oil could be easily pressed out of them. Today, we associate sesame oil with oriental cuisine as it is common in Chinese, Japanese, and other Asian styles of cooking. Toasted sesame oil is intensely flavored, providing a considerable amount of flavor for a small quantity of oil.

Corn oil is one of the most common vegetable oils, particularly here in the United States where over 70 percent of the world's supply is produced. Nearly all corn oil is refined before being sold, and the refined oil retains a hint of the flavor of corn and a characteristic yellow hue. It is an excellent general-purpose cooking oil. Unrefined corn oil is becoming increasingly available and is absolutely delicious, full of the aroma and taste of fresh corn. Although only a small quantity is produced, it is fairly inexpensive.

Canola oil—or, more accurately, rapeseed oil—is currently enjoying great popularity and is characterized by its lack of any particular flavor. It is praised for being low in saturated fats (6 percent) and relatively high in monounsaturates (60 percent), and for containing omega-3 essential fatty acids (10 percent). Rapeseed oil does contain the toxic erucic acid. What is called canola oil is a Canadian (hence, canola) strain of the plant that has had most of the acid bred out. Food experts say there is no danger, although the controversy continues.

Other seed oils, such as grape, safflower, and sunflower oils, are mild in taste and have a high smoke point, which makes them ideal for high-temperature cooking. Grapeseed oil is used infrequently in this country and tends to be fairly expensive when you do find it. Cottonseed oil, once commonly used in commercial food production, must be refined to be comestible, has no special qualities to recommend it, and is low in nutrients. It is one of the oils used in generic vegetable oils. Because it contains the highest level of residual pesticides of any of the edible oils, it is best avoided.

Produced primarily in California, avocado oil is extracted from the fruit not the seed of the avocado. It is an expensive oil, a fact that limits its value as a general cooking oil, in spite of its high smoke point. It is high in mono-unsaturated fatty acids, making it a healthy choice. The oil does not, however, retain a great deal of characteristic flavor.

Oil made from pumpkin seeds is particularly delicious, especially if the seeds have been toasted. It is low in saturated fats (9 percent) and very high in the omega-6 fatty acid, and is considered one of the healthier oils. It is, however, extremely difficult to find in this country. I have seen it only in France. If you find it, keep in mind that it should not be heated, just used in vinaigrettes or as a flavoring agent to finish a dish.

Two vegetable seeds, coconut and palm, yield oils that are exceptionally high in saturated fats. These two oils are used extensively in commercial food production, largely because they are inexpensive. Both oils are used in the production of margarine, in many commercial baked products, and in the production of blended vegetable or salad oils.

NUT OILS

For a nut oil to have its characteristic flavor and aroma, the nuts must be roasted. Oils made from unroasted nuts are flavorless; they are used for various purposes, but rarely for cooking. Oils made from good-quality nuts that have been roasted with care offer a vast range of flavors and culinary possibilities. The most flavorful nut oils, pressed from hazelnuts and walnuts, are produced in Europe. Because walnut trees thrive where olive trees do not, the regional cuisines of certain areas of France and Italy are rich with the oil of the walnut. Vinaigrettes made with walnut oil and sauces featuring walnuts abound. If olive oil is the oil of the Mediterranean, walnut oil has long been known as the oil of France. In her book *The Cooking of South-West France,*

Paula Wolfert tells of several old mills that are still making startlingly delicious walnut oils by the old method. One of them, in Sainte Nathalène, near Sarlat in the Dordogne, is over one hundred years old. The walnuts are cracked open and gently crushed by a stream-driven mill. After crushing, the nuts are heated in a wooden caldron to 120 degrees F. The oil is then pressed out directly into the 150 quart bottles the mill produces twice a week. If you find yourself in Bordeaux, you can buy this oil at: M. Gouraud, 7 place des Capucins (telephone (56) 91 65 31).

Nearly all of the small quantity of specialty nut oil currently produced in this country is refined, the natural aromas and flavors being eliminated during the process. Even after refining, these oils have a low smoke point, so there is little reason to use most of them. An exception is the walnut oil made by Loriva Supreme Foods, Inc., which is full of the flavor of walnuts. With the increasing demand, other domestic brands may soon improve. The two draw-backs to the European brands are cost—they are generally expensive—and freshness. Because they are so expensive, they frequently spend too much time on the market shelf. They are sensitive, unstable oils that become rancid more quickly than do most other oils. If you find you have purchased one with an unpleasant taste, return it to your merchant. Peanut oil is probably the most familiar of the nut oils. In its refined form, it has just a slight hint of peanut flavor and is one of the most commonly used oils, the choice of many chefs whose specialties include Creole, Cajun, and oriental cuisines. Unrefined, it has a long and pleasant aftertaste of raw peanuts. Almond oil, because it retains a strong taste of almonds, is used most frequently in baking. Although it has a high smoke point, it is not widely used in general cooking. In recent years, oils from pine nuts and pistachio nuts have been produced. They are, however, not widely available, and are extremely expensive. Both oils are intensely flavored, with a distinctive scent and taste, and should be used sparingly. The pine nut oil is pale, and the pistachio nut oil is a rich, deep green.

OLIVE OIL—THE GOLDEN GLORY OF CIVILIZATION

O Love! what hours were thine and mine,
In lands of palm and southern pine;
*   In lands of palm, of orange-blossom,*
Of olive, aloe, and maize and vine!
        Alfred, Lord Tennyson,
        The Daisy

When I returned from my first trip to Italy, made in the spring of 1990, I was laden with several liters of golden-green olive oil from Chianti. I hobbled onto the plane, trying to appear as if my carry-on luggage actually met the weight requirement. I am lucky that the overhead compartment did not collapse and drown me in a rich bath of olive oil. Those precious bottles made it back intact and were my balm and my solace in the days following my return when all I wanted to do was head back over the Atlantic. Instead, I ate grilled bread drizzled with the best of the olive oil, drank red wine, and longed for Tuscany where olive trees anoint the countryside with their rustic, silvery beauty.

An olive branch placed above the door will drive away evil spirits and keep husbands faithful, the Spanish say.

Olive oil is not the only oil in the world, of course, but is in my opinion the best and the most interesting. Setting out on my research, I was guided by curiosity, not by personal affinity; what I discovered affirmed my particular passion. No other oil engages the emotions, or evokes such reverence, as the oil, or juice, of the olive. Darrell Corti, an importer of specialty foods and authority on olive oils, says that "olive oil is interesting because it is very special; in fact, it is sacred, probably more sacred than wine. It was used for anointing, for light, for flavoring."

THE FIRST OLIVE TREE *The first olive tree is said to have been planted during a dispute between Athene and Poseidon for the possession of the Acropolis. Athene claimed that she could give greater benefits to her people. Poseidon, when he struck a rock with his trident and a spring began to flow, hoped to prove her wrong. She planted an olive tree beside the spring, the gods acknowledged her gift, and she kept possession of the temple. Thus the first olive tree grew at the center of the Acropolis in the center of Athens, the very heart of Greek civilization.*

Olive oil is sacred, infused with spiritual qualities by religions throughout the world. It is the ritual oil of the Catholic Church, where it is blessed in a special mass each year. Olive oil was used to anoint Queen Elizabeth II, the baptized infant nephew of Michael Corleone in *The Godfather*, and President John Kennedy as he lay stricken in Parkland Hospital in Dallas in 1963. It has been used throughout the ages in religious ceremonies and rituals and to provide illumination in the dark of night. No other oil has such a scope of meaning, or such a spectrum of flavor, which is influenced by the subtle variations in the variety of seed, the soil in which it has grown, the climate, and, according to some, the temperament of the producer.

YOU TAKE OLIVES AND YOU PRESS THEM

Part of the beauty of olive oil is its simplicity, and its perfection in its natural state. As Darrell Corti says, you take olives and you press them, a fact that has led to the comment that olive oil is found, not made. It is a little more complex than that, but not much, for olive oil is simply the juice of the olive, at its best when it is first pressed out of the fruit. Many factors influence the outcome of the oil, beginning with the variety of the fruit used. The large Mission olives most common to the American table yield little oil and it is usually of poor quality. The best oil olives are small.

Production of olive oil begins with the harvest, the timing of which is a major factor in the final product. The picking of the olives starts as early as September, when the olives are underripe and still green. They yield little oil, but their flavor is intense. Oil from olives harvested early has a low percentage of acid and the characteristic deep green color we identify in many of the oils from Tuscany, where the most robust oils are produced. Some olives are harvested in the red-ripe stage and blended with the earlier harvested oil to create a more balanced product. In general, the oils from fruit that is harvested in the black-ripe stage are of inferior quality, containing more acid and less flavor. The value of ripe olives is that they contain more oil, though it must be refined to become palatable.

The traditional method of harvesting is slow and time-consuming. The youngest green olives must be picked off the branches, whereas riper olives can be beaten or shaken down and collected in nets strung beneath the trees. Black-ripe olives frequently drop to the ground and are bruised. These olives may be the easiest to gather, but their taste is impaired, not only by their overripeness, but also by the bruising.

Olives are stored for a few days before being pressed, during which time some of the water in the fruit evaporates. It is essential that care is taken during the storage period to keep the olives cool. If they are piled high, their temperature will rise and they will begin to ferment, which is fatal to the production of oil. The best producers spread their olives in thin layers to prevent the buildup of heat. If olives are left resting for too long, they develop higher acid and unpleasant odors and flavors. The resulting oil must be refined after pressing.

Cultivars of the olive, Olea europaea, *are numerous, being found wherever the common olive is grown. Those in California came with the Spanish missionaries. One olive grower in Sonoma County, north of San Francisco, is importing seedlings from Italy in the hope of producing olive oils as good as those of Tuscany.*

California:	Mission, Manzanilla, Sevillano
Italy:	Frantoio, Moraiolo, Leccino, Agogia, Rosciolo, Raggia, Nicastrese, Biancolilla, Coratina
Spain:	Arbequina, Manzanillo, Sevillano, Lechin, Gordal, Picual, Racimal, Argudell, Verdillo, Nevadillo blanco, Blanqueta, Hojiblanca, Rojal
France:	Olivière, Pigalle, Pendoulier, Cailletier, Moiral, Picholine, Lucques, Niçoise, La Tanche
Greece:	Caronaiki, Daphnoelia, Mouratolia, Carydolia, Stravolia, Kalamata
Portugal:	Gallego, Verdeal, Cordovil, Carrasquenha, Redondil, Madural
Libya:	Enduri, R'ghiani, Rasli
Tunisia:	Ouslati, Meski, Cornicabra
Turkey:	Sam, Girit, Hurma

The simplest method of crushing olives is with a granite stone, and there are several ancient types remaining, some of them still in use throughout the Mediterranean region. Larger producers still using this method have their own stones; the small farmer usually takes his olives to a central location to be crushed and pressed. After crushing, the pulp is layered on nylon mats, which are stacked several high, with metal disks between the layers. The mats of olive pulp are then subjected to several tons of pressure from a screw or hydraulic press. The best oil from the finest olives is placed in a holding tank and left to settle for a few weeks before being ladled into jars, bottles, crocks, or urns.

Most oils go through further processing. The oil must be separated from the water in the fruit, and it is quicker to centrifuge the water out than it is to let the olive oil rise to the top of a large container. Many larger factories may use

heat and water to facilitate the extraction process, though the resulting oil must be refined.

Fresh olive oil must be allowed to settle so that the minute particles of fruit can precipitate out of the liquid. These particles form the sediment we see in the bottom of an unfiltered oil. Although filtering is not essential if the oil is truly of high quality, nearly all oils are filtered, the best through cotton. Some experts on olive oil feel that filtered oils look more attractive and claim that the particles present in unfiltered oil speed deterioration. Others make the opposite claims. It is really a matter of individual preference. I find the sight of a bottle of the cloudy green liquid exciting, because I know the delightful possibilities within.

This time-consuming, traditional method of production, with its hand-picking, stone-crushing, and natural settling, is quickly being replaced by the new horizontal decanter method, a continuous system of production that some advocates—especially those who use it—claim results in a finer oil. Certainly, the possibility of contamination by odors in the air or by a worker's unclean hands is eliminated. (Olive oil is unstable and will pick up scents in the room where it is made. This presented a problem in the days when the large stone presses were driven by horses. Today the entire process can take place away from such potential influences, away from light, away from any possible interference.) The process can result in high-quality oils, especially if the oils are blended, to ensure that they are consistent. Critics of the horizontal decanter method of production point out that, inevitably, pits and leaves are crushed in the process and contribute to the final taste of the oil. I wonder, too, how much character can we expect from all that stainless steel, from that clinically sterile room? What is the temperament of the machinery? What do we lose as we become more efficient?

VARIETIES OF OLIVE OILS

THE VIRGINITY OF OLIVE OIL   *European labeling requirements base the distinction among levels of virginity—extra, superfine, fine, and virgin—solely on acidity. The first cold pressing of superior olives yields an oil of low acidity, but the oleic acid level of any inferior oil can be lowered by chemical refining. Large companies frequently sell as extra virgin a refined oil to which some first-pressed oil has been added for flavor, a practice that is completely legal, but nonetheless deceptive.*

Extra virgin olive oil—*Less than 1 percent oleic acid*
Superfine virgin olive oil—*Between 1.01 percent and 1.50 percent oleic acid*
Fine virgin olive oil—*1.51 percent to 3 percent oleic acid*
Virgin olive oil—*3.1 percent to 4 percent oleic acid*
Lamp oil—*Over 4 percent oleic acid; not comestible*
Olive oil (also called Pure)—*Rectified and refined lamp oil with up to 10 percent virgin olive oil added*
Sansa oil (also called Pomace oil, pit oil)—*Rectified and refined olive oil extracted from the pulp of the first and second pressings with up to 10 percent virgin olive oil added for taste.*

From *The Feast of the Olive* by Maggie Blyth Klein (Reading, Mass.: Aris Books/Addison-Wesley, 1983).

The United States recognizes two grades of olive oil: virgin and pure. Virgin olive oil must be extracted by purely mechanical means with no further processing and with a level of acidity no greater than 3 percent. Pure olive oil is refined, 100 percent olive oil.

Determining true quality among olive oils is difficult for the consumer. Because of the ambiguity in labeling requirements, ferreting out an authentic extra virgin oil from among the industrially produced oils is not a simple task, although there are a few guidelines that help. First of all, keep in mind that it is the smaller farmers who are making oil in the traditional manner of simply removing the juice from the fruit with a stone press. Because of the time-consuming process and limited production, these true extra virgin olive oils are expensive. That consideration immediately rules out, for authenticity, any inexpensive oil labeled as "extra virgin." Price is, however, no longer a guarantee of quality in olive oil. Larger producers, cultivating the lucrative gourmet market, are selling inferior oils that have been refined and bolstered with the addition of some cold-pressed oil at high prices. Some of these oils are perfectly satisfactory; a few have a pleasing taste of olives and an acceptable texture; the best have their place in a pantry, where they should be used when the flavor of olive oil is necessary but will not be the dominant factor. Some are unpleasant, bland, oily, and occasionally even rancid.

The true extra virgin olive oils—the specialty oils from Tuscany, Liguria, Provence, and Spain—should be treated more as a condiment, so that their lush flavor and texture will be highlighted. The best resource for these oils is a reliable retail market and a trusted merchant who will guarantee his products and lead you to the best.

TESTING FOR TRUE VIRGINITY *Place a small quantity of the oil in a glass bowl and refrigerate it for a few days. If it becomes crystalline, the chances are good that it is a true extra virgin olive oil. If it forms a block, it is most likely chemically refined oil that has had some first-pressed oil added. A buttery consistency indicates pit, or sansa, oil.*

OLIVE OIL AND HEALTH

In the ancient world, olive oil was used on wounds to promote healing, for cleansing the skin, and for soothing it after the burning and drying effects of sun and wind. It was used on hair to make it shine and was taken as a tonic for many ills, including insomnia, nausea, and ulcers. Many of these ancient treatments have stayed with us, evolving into folk remedies that are still used in many parts of the world. Olive oil is said to prevent dandruff and wrinkles. There are even claims that olive oil slows the aging processes of both the brain and the body's internal tissues and organs. The golden glory of civilization, olive oil has been used since earliest time to enhance life on all levels. Today, we know it best for its marvelous culinary properties and the current claims made about its health benefits.

With growing concern over heart disease, scientists have examined those cultures where incidence is low. It is common knowledge now that the Mediterranean diet has produced an extremely low rate of coronary disease in that region, especially compared with rates in Northern Europe and the United States of America. The areas with the lowest incidence of heart disease and cancer are those where the diet is closest to what it has been for millennia, when 80 percent of a day's calories came from grains and olive oil. Americans, on average, get 70 percent of their calories from animal fats and protein, with a large portion of those fats made up of saturated fatty acids.

Olive oil is about 82 percent monounsaturated fatty acid. Simply put, that means that olive oil may lower the level of low-density lipoproteins without lowering the level of high-density lipoproteins, which are essential to our health. Because polyunsaturated oils lower both HDLs and LDLs, it is now generally considered that monounsaturates are the healthier choice.

Health claims about particular foodstuffs can be both overwhelming and confusing, and it seems to be part of the American spirit to embrace fad after fad, abandoning one for the next to come along with its miraculous claims. Olive oil has the blessing of the ages.

FLAVORED OILS

Oils with some sort of added flavoring agent are becoming increasingly popular, with numerous types available in the marketplace. In most instances, it is a good idea—for both taste and economy—to make your own. When purchasing commercially flavored oils, one pays a great deal for the additional flavor, and it is hard to determine what types of raw materials have been used. An elaborately packaged oil with a beautiful sprig of thyme will not be cheap, but in fact may be made from inexpensive products, such as refined olive oil and dried herbs. Seasoned oils for popcorn or wok cooking are expensive but inferior and often full of dried and artificial flavorings. A few of the flavored oils on the market, notably the fiery *diavolicchio*, a hot pepper olive oil from Italy, and *pumate*, a sun-dried tomato olive oil from San Remo, are superior products. *Fortunati*, from Italy, offers another newly available flavored oil that is gaining a great deal of notice among chefs and restaurant diners. It is an olive oil infused with the aroma of white truffles and is truly spectacular. In Italy, one often finds herb-infused olive oils on the tables in better restaurants. The oils are used as condiments, adding a splash of flavor and aroma. Some of these Italian oils are just making it into our country and many of them are excellent, far superior to domestic brands of flavored oils, which tend to be of questionable quality and poor flavor. As they become more widely available, and perhaps less costly, they will offer excellent culinary possibilities.

With the exception of these few specialty oils, I rarely use flavored or seasoned oils, but that does not mean that you should not. Because I have never cared for the quality of infused oils that have been available, I prefer to use a pure oil and add spices and herbs fresh when I am cooking. If you prefer your oils scented, it is a simple process and, for the most part, entirely safe. There is some slight danger of botulism if you wish to add garlic to an oil that will remain at room temperature, but you can take certain precautions to prevent any possibility of catastrophe. First of all, avoid using chopped garlic. Use whole cloves that have been scored or cut in half and soaked in vinegar for a day. Remove the garlic from the vinegar, dry it, place it in your oil, and you will have no need to worry about botulism.

You may introduce other flavoring agents, fresh and dried herbs, spices, lemon peel, and so on, into cold oil with impunity. Heating the ingredients before combining them will create a risk of botulism in addition to destroying much of the flavor you are hoping to achieve. When you use fresh herbs, you will find that the flavor deteriorates rapidly and that bubbles form on the surface of the oil. This is lactic acid bacteria, and, although it poses no health risks, the higher the moisture content of your flavoring agents, the more quickly they will reproduce, often destroying the taste of your oil in just a day or two. Because the bacteria give off a terrible taste, oils combined with fresh herbs have a short life. Make them in small batches, keep them refrigerated to slow the reproduction of the bacteria, and discard them after a week to ten days, or sooner if their taste deteriorates.

ESSENTIAL OILS

Some culinary oils are used, not for their cooking properties, nor for their ability to transfer heat or lubricate pieces of food, but for the flavors they impart. These are the essential oils, lemon oil, for example, or bitter orange oil. They are pure oils removed from their source material by a process of distillation, extraction, or expression. They impart concentrated aromas and flavors and are used widely in baking and in other types of cooking to impart an intensity of flavor to foods in which a juice would not be appropriate.

OIL TASTING

It is important to be familiar with the taste of the oils that you use, and to know the best ways of tasting and evaluating a variety of oils. This will give you more control over the final results of your recipes and a better intuitive sense of which products to use. Most of us are not in the habit of opening the cupboard for a little nip of oil, so the process of tasting needs some explaining. On pages 244–246 are tasting forms on which you can describe characteristics of specific oils and note your likes and dislikes. Tasting oils is hard work for our palates, and I do not recommend that you taste more than seven or eight at one time. Two or three are enough for the novice.

To taste an oil, pour a small quantity into a clear glass—a wineglass works perfectly. Smell the oil and note the aroma. Rub a little into the back of your hand and smell it again. Can you identify the raw material from which the oil was made? It will be most noticeable in unrefined oils, but many refined oils do have a lingering hint of the grain, nut, seed, or fruit from whence they came. Pour a small quantity of oil onto a plastic spoon, take it into your mouth, and hold it there briefly, breathing in slightly. As you swallow it, note the way it slides down the throat and the degree to which it coats the tongue. Between tastings, cleanse the palate with a celery stick or a piece of bread and a drink of mineral water. If the consumption of oil by the spoonful is particularly objectionable to you, soak a cube of bread in the oil and then taste it. It will not yield as immediate a taste of the oil, but the method is preferred by some.

A good-quality oil will not be overly oily nor coat the tongue with fat. It will have a pleasing, fresh taste and a rich texture. If an oil is rancid, you should be able to detect it immediately. It will have an off taste, something that is obviously unpleasant that cannot be ascribed to individual preference. Rancid oils are often described as having a painty smell and a scratchy taste. They can produce gastrointestinal discomfort similar to that caused by foods cooked in overheated oil. Such oils should be discarded or, if recently purchased, returned to the market for a refund.

With oils other than olive oils, tasting is a matter of acquainting oneself with the characteristics of a particular oil. An interesting exercise is to taste an unused refined oil, a refined oil that has been used for deep frying and cooled, and an unrefined oil—all made from the same raw material—and note the differences in aroma and taste. You should look for quality and character, not merely interesting variation or nuance. Hazelnut oil, for example, should taste clean with a long finish of hazelnut flavor. In any unrefined oil, there should be a clean, bright presence of the raw material. One of the results of tasting a variety of oils in this way is that they become part of our store of culinary knowledge, waiting in our mind's palate to present themselves at just the right moment. It is one of the ways in which we can become better intuitive cooks, able to navigate the culinary world without specific recipes to guide us.

Because of the diversity of olive oils, tasting them is much more complex than tasting other oils. It is extra virgin olive oils that we taste for variations in flavor and style, and one can approach the subject in a variety of ways. You can taste several olive oils within a narrow price range, for example, an informative lesson on cost and quality. Or you can taste one olive oil from each major country of production, though it must be determined that they are of comparable quality. There is no sense in comparing an inferior Spanish oil with a superior French oil. You can compare the major brands, or a variety of oils from small farmers in a single region. If only a few extra virgin olive oils are available in your area, you might arrange a tasting that includes all available olive oils. Each participant provides one oil, and everyone is able to discover a preference for a nominal cost.

If you are especially fond of olive oils, it makes sense to taste them regularly. Preferences for olive oil are very subjective. You will probably find your preferences changing as you become more knowledgeable. Flavors can vary from year to year, and your favorite brand one year may not be your favorite the next. The heartier, more robust oils can be a shock to a palate that has known only refined vegetable oils. Once the shock is over, a delightful new world of possibilities opens up.

Experts on olive oil can discover a panorama of details about an oil from a single taste. The type of olive is indicated by the color, and the first sip frequently reveals the country and region of origin, whether or not the oil is truly extra virgin, and if it is made by a small or large producer. An experienced taster can also tell if leaves of the olive tree made it into the crush. Even these experts exhaust their palates after tasting seven or eight oils.

In spite of the importance of personal preferences, the

oils from certain regions of the world are recognized as superior. Most experts claim that the best oils come from Provence, Liguria, or Tuscany, though there is every indication that some of the oils from Spain will soon be contenders. The Provencal oils are known as the "lady oils," being more subtle and elegant than the heartier Tuscan oils, which have more body and a more rustic character. The Ligurian oils are delicate and are said to have more finesse.

MENU FOR AN OLIVE OIL TASTING

For each taster provide:

1 plastic spoon, several celery sticks, cubes of sourdough bread, a large glass of unflavored mineral water, evaluation forms, and a pencil.

On the common table place:

The bottles of olive oil to be tasted, eight-ounce wineglasses to be filled with between one and two inches of each oil, the glasses being arranged in front of their corresponding bottles, and extra bottles of chilled mineral water.

COOKING TECHNIQUES

THE SECOND TIME AROUND You can get a little more life out of your deep-frying oil by straining it through a coffee filter after it has cooled. This will work only if the oil has been kept below its smoke point and has not been used to fry salted, spiced, or breaded foods. You should be able to get a second frying out of a batch of oil cleaned in this way.

DEEP-FRYING

One of the main culinary functions of oils is as an agent for the transfer of heat. A portion of food submerged into a liquid that is uniformly heated is cooked more evenly and consistently than a portion placed in a dry pan or on a grill. Oil can be taken to a high temperature, and food submerged in it is cooked evenly throughout, and more quickly than if it were cooked by circulating hot air or by direct contact with a heated surface. The process is ideally suited for certain foods.

There are simple guidelines for proper cooking in oil, and some oils are better-suited for the process than others. First of all, it is important to understand and be familiar with the smoke points of the various oils. The term *smoke point* refers to the temperature at which a fat breaks down into visible gaseous products. The quantities of free fatty acids in a fat influence this temperature, and vegetable oils with their lower fatty acids content have a higher smoke point, around 450 degrees F., than animal fats, which smoke at around 375 degrees F. One of the reasons it is essential to cook with fresh oil is that contamination with food particles lowers the smoke point.

Deep-frying should always be done with refined oils. First of all, the taste of unrefined oils is destroyed by higher temperatures, making the added expense unnecessary and wasteful. More importantly, because of the presence of particulate matter, unrefined oils have lower and variable smoke points, making them unsuitable for the process. The importance of keeping oils below their optimum temperatures is not just aesthetic. As an oil reaches its smoke point, it begins to decompose, and glycerol is converted into acrolein, the irritant responsible for the gastrointestinal discomfort associated with eating greasy foods.

Smoke Points of Common Culinary Oils

TYPE OF OIL	SMOKE POINT	SUITABLE COOKING METHODS OR USES
ALMOND	495°F.	Dressings, grilled fish
AVOCADO	520°F.	Dressings; too expensive for frying
CANOLA (rapeseed)	437°F.	Frying, deep-frying, sautéing
COCONUT	Not available	Not recommended for cooking
CORN, refined	410°F.	Frying, baking, sautéing
CORN, unrefined	250°F.	Flavoring, dressings, emulsions
COTTONSEED	450°F.	Not recommended for cooking
GRAPESEED	446°F.	Deep-frying, frying, sautéing
HAZELNUT	Not available	Dressings, sauces, flavoring
MUSTARD	Not available	Dressings, flavoring
OLIVE, extra virgin	250°F.	Dressings, flavoring, emulsions, condiment
OLIVE, pure refined	410°F.	Frying, sautéing, baking
PEANUT (ground nut)	450°F.	Frying, deep-frying, emulsions, roux
PUMPKIN SEED	224°F.	Dressings, flavoring
RICE BRAN	500°F.	Too expensive for general use
SAFFLOWER	450°F.	Deep-frying, frying
SESAME	410°F.	Flavoring, stir-frying, sautéing
SOYBEAN	450°F.	Not recommended for frying: It foams at high temperatures
SUNFLOWER	392°F.	Frying, sautéing
WALNUT	Not available	Dressings, sauces, flavoring, light sautéing

Sources: *Bailey's Industrial Oil & Fat Products,* 4th ed., 1979; and *Spectrum Natural Kitchen Guide,* 1990.

FIVE RULES FOR SUCCESSFUL
DEEP-FRYING

1. *Heat the oil to the proper temperature: The temperature should be 350°F. unless otherwise stated. Fry the food in batches small enough so as not to lower the temperature of the oil drastically. If the temperature is too low, oil will seep into the batter instead of sealing it and you will have mushy fried foods. If foods brown too quickly, the inside crust will be gummy and the food will not be cooked properly. Properly browned foods will be properly cooked inside, too. Remember to return the oil to the correct temperature after each batch of frying.*

2. *Use fresh, unused oil: Oil contaminated with salt, bits of batter, water, juices, or other substances loses its ability to seal the breading or batter of foods.*

3. *Use enough oil to submerge completely whatever is being fried.*

4. *Do not bread or batter foods for frying until just before placing them in the oil. Liquids from the food will leach out, making the coating gummy and unpleasant.*

5. *Do not overcrowd the pan: Make sure the portions of food being fried are not touching one another and are completely surrounded by the cooking oil.*

There is no reason to use expensive, specialty oils for deep-frying. Their flavors begin to break down well below the needed temperature. Some chefs prefer the slight nutty flavor offered by peanut oil; others prefer the more neutral-tasting safflower or corn oils. Some people prefer to cook exclusively with olive oil and find the lower priced, mild-tasting pure olive oils perfectly acceptable for deep-frying. It was once thought that olive oil had a much lower smoke point than other vegetable oils, but that is now known to be untrue.

SAUTÉING

The process of sautéing, also known as pan-frying, is very simple: Small or medium-sized pieces of food are cooked quickly in a hot pan with a small quantity of fat, either butter or other animal fat, or oil. The word "sauté" comes from the French *sauter*, to jump, which refers to the continual agitation of the pan that keeps the food in motion, or jumping, so that it will not brown too quickly.

Although clarified butter is the traditional cooking medium in this process, any oil with a medium-high smoke point can be used. To cut down on animal fat but retain the richness of the clarified butter, use a mixture of butter and oil. The pan and its fats should be heated before the food—which should be at room temperature—is added.

Deglazing the pan is an excellent way to make use of the flavors that have accumulated in the pan after the food has cooked. Simply remove the food from the pan to a warmed serving dish or platter, add a small quantity of liquid—stock, wine, or vinegar—and swirl the liquid to pick up the juices and particles stuck to the pan. Reduce the sauce, pour it over the cooked food, and serve it immediately. Several recipes cooked in this way and using both oil and vinegar are included in the recipe section.

STIR-FRYING

A technique adopted from oriental cuisine, stir-frying has become increasingly popular in the United States. As concerns with health have grown, Americans have been eating more fresh vegetables and looking for better ways of preparing them. The quick, light results of stir-frying are particularly appealing. Stir-frying is done in a wok or other thin, conical pan, most frequently with a supporting metal ring, though it is not essential when used over gas heat. Only a small quantity of cooking oil is needed. Some vegetables also need a small quantity of liquid; stock, soy sauce, or Thai fish sauce are frequently added. Sesame oil may be used for flavoring in stir-frying, as may certain scented oils and vinegars—especially those flavored with ginger or garlic.

Although the cooking process is quick in this method, preparation of the food can be time-consuming. The vegetables and meats to be cooked are sliced into small, uniform pieces. They are then cooked in batches so that all will be at the proper stage of doneness when the dish is complete. Virtually any meats and vegetables can be combined into a good stir-fry, making formal recipes unnecessary for this technique, which is why I have included none in this book. Do experiment until you find your own favorite combinations (or refer to the bibliography for references to helpful cookbooks).

PART TWO

All About Vinegar

VINEGAR IS UBIQUITOUS. IT APPEARS IN NEARLY every pantry cupboard the world over, although the shape of its container, its type and flavor, its regulation and uses change with its location. Vinegar is one of those ingredients that is generally taken for granted, so universal is its use in recipes. Like salt or pepper or sugar, you will rarely find it indexed in a cookbook, or if you do, the index will probably contain only a few of the recipes of which it is an integral part. Vinaigrettes will appear, as will vinegar pie or fruit vinegars perhaps, but vinegar will have made its aromatic, acidic appearance in many more recipes than those listed.

Because vinegar has been available for so long, it is not something we tend to think about too much. I believe an understanding of vinegar, what it is exactly and what variables influence its production, is important to anyone interested in food. Once that basic overview has been made, one can choose comfortably among the many vinegars available in the marketplace, or make an intelligent effort to produce vinegar at home.

WHAT IS VINEGAR?

All types of vinegar must contain a minimum of four grams of acetic acid per 100 cubic centimeters and all must be a product of alcoholic fermentation and the subsequent acetic fermentation of one of the following liquids:

The juice of apples: vinegar, cider vinegar, apple cider vinegar
The juice of grapes: wine vinegar
An infusion of barley malt or cereals, the starch in which has been converted by malt: malt vinegar
Sugar syrup or refiner's syrup: sugar vinegar
A solution of glucose or dextrose: glucose vinegar
Dilute distilled alcohol: spirit, distilled, or grain vinegar

> (Source: University of California, College of Agriculture, Circular 334, January 1934.)

Simply put, vinegar is the by-product of the action of a single species of bacteria upon alcohol. In the presence of oxygen, acetobacters digest the alcohol in a liquid, producing acetic acid, which gives vinegar its characteristic sour taste.

Our word "vinegar" comes from the French, *vinaigre*, which means, literally, sour wine: *vin aigre*. In the United States, the name derived from the literal translation can legally be used only if the substrate is the juice of apples. In Italy, vinegar is known as *aceto*, named for the bacteria that produce it rather than for the results of production.

Wine is one of the primary substrates for vinegar, used in those parts of the world where it is widely consumed. In fact, if you know the types of fermented alcohol indigenous to an area, you can make an educated guess about the type of vinegar you might find there. The English, a beer- and cider-drinking people, use malt vinegar and cider vinegar considerably more than they use wine vinegars. In Italy wine vinegars are predominant. Spain is well known for both its fortified wines and its sherry vinegars. Not surpris-

ingly, champagne vinegar, white wine vinegar, and red wine vinegar are all common in France. Malt vinegar reappears in the cuisines of Germany and eastern Europe where beer has long been a favored beverage. Japan, not surprisingly, makes extensive use of rice vinegar, acidic companion to their well-known *sake*, an intoxicating beverage made from fermented rice.

HISTORY

By the time humans began making a written record of their activities, vinegar had been a part of life for a long time. Some of the first written records refer to date wine and date vinegar as being common in Babylonia as long ago as 5000 B.C. Because the production of alcohol and acetic acid occurs naturally, it seems safe to speculate that vinegar was around long before that. Its actual discovery was probably accidental: Someone tasted a liquid, some wine left uncovered, perhaps, or a syrup that had fermented out in the open, and sensed the culinary possibilities, however crude they might have been when human culture was so young. But there is evidence that commercial production was extensive by 2000 B.C., and that the addition of flavoring agents—herbs, spices, and fruits—was common practice.

Throughout history, vinegar has had medicinal as well as culinary uses. It has served as an elixir and as a tonic in times of poor health. Vinegar was extremely valuable as a preservative before modern methods of refrigeration were developed and is still essential for canning and pickling.

- *Tobacco odors can be eliminated by placing a bowl of white distilled vinegar in the offending room.*
- *To remove lime deposits from your teakettle, fill it with half a cup distilled vinegar and gently boil it for twenty minutes. Rinse it well before using.*
- *A teaspoon of vinegar can save an overly salty soup, sauce, or stew. Simply stir in the vinegar and a teaspoon of sugar.*
- *A teaspoon of vinegar in the poaching water will help keep eggs well formed. Tie the flavor of the vinegar to other flavors in the meal.*
- *Regret that bumper sticker you put on in the fervor of the moment? A few applications of white vinegar should remove it.*

HOW VINEGAR IS MADE

Although vinegar has been actively produced for thousands of years, the first modern method of commercial production began in France about five hundred years ago in the city of Orleans, after which the method takes its name. The Orleans process, or slow method as it is also called, was the only way vinegar was produced commercially until the development of the generator method by Hermann Boerhaave, a Dutch technologist. The Orleans method is slow because as the substrate sits in its barrel only a small surface area is exposed to oxygen. The acetobacters act slowly to digest the alcohol. Few commercial vinegar producers still use the old, slow method, although those that do are heralded by food critics and chefs as offering a superior product. There is no heat involved in the Orleans method, so the subtle flavors of the original material are not destroyed. But because the producers of Orleans-style vinegars are aiming for quality, part of the difference in their products can be attributed to the superior raw ingredients they begin with and the care that goes into production.

One company that does use the process, the Kimberley Wine Vinegar Works of San Francisco, makes its vinegars with Chardonnay and Cabernet Sauvignon wines. After aged wine is inoculated with an actively fermenting vinegar and a mother (see page 49) purchased from a laboratory is added, the solution sits in barrels for approximately five months to ferment until the acidity reaches 6.5 percent. It is then bottled and corked. This process, from the time the wine is purchased until the vinegar is bottled and sold, can take as long as two and a half years.

> 'Tis melancholy, and a fearful sign
>   Of human fraility, folly, also crime,
> That love and marriage rarely can combine,
>   Although they both are born in the same clime;
> Marriage from love, live vinegar from wine—
>   A sad, sour, sober beverage—by time
> Is sharpen'd from its high celestial flavor,
> Down to a very homely household savor.
>   Lord Byron, *Don Juan*

There were two problems with the early Orleans method of production. One was that it was inherently slow, a problem for which there is no solution save patience. The other was more urgent. Frequently the vinegar mother would grow to an enormous size in the vinegar barrel, crowding the vinegar and oxygen and slowing production. The formation of a thick mother can still be a problem today, although most producers seek strains of bacteria that have a minimal tendency to form a mother. In 1868 Louis Pasteur perfected a method of keeping the mother afloat with a wooden raft. Although Pasteur may not have realized it at the time, this technique would result in a superior vinegar. A submerged mother is essentially dead and contributes a taste of decay to the vinegar.

Because the Orleans method is slow, it was inevitable that new methods would be developed. The generator process, the first to offer an alternative to the slow method, is a technique by which the vinegar is dripped or manipulated in some way to increase the surface area exposed to oxygen so that the acetobacters feed upon the alcohol more quickly. When the process was first developed, a variety of structures were made to facilitate it, but all had a similar function. Some sort of material—frequently wood shavings or branches, but charcoal, corn cobs, chunks of pottery, and various other materials were used—was packed into an enclosed cylinder.

The original generator, or fast, method of production has evolved into a completely automated process that converts the substrate into vinegar in about twenty-four hours. The Frings acetator has brought speed and efficiency to the vinegar industry and is currently used for most commercial vinegar production. In a highly aerobic environment, the substrate is kept at the optimum temperature for the function of the acetobacters, and the level of acidity is closely monitored.

Other techniques are used for various specialty and varietal vinegars, but it is not necessary to understand the nuances of the methods to enjoy the culinary possibilities of the products.

MAKING VINEGAR AT HOME

The making of vinegar at home is a controversial subject. "Don't do it," most experts advise. But what of the many celebrated chefs who say that they collect their leftover wine in a barrel and, romantically, it becomes in a few short months the best vinegar they have ever tasted? A friend crushes pears and quinces, places them in a big crock, covers them, and months later has, *voila!*, wonderful fruit vinegar. Methods for producing vinegar at home and in restaurants not only vary widely but also appear to break all of the rules, using, as they do, mothers that are dead or additional wine in midprocess, which will disturb the forming mother and cause it to sink. You can conclude that there is an element of magic, of alchemy, of the gifted personal touch at work here. Certainly, it is not a process that lends itself to methodical description.

The process is, at best, unpredictable and, according to Dr. George York, a food technologist at the University of California at Davis, does not often yield satisfactory results.

Another problem with vinegar made at home is that it is extremely difficult to measure the acidity, which is frequently very low. Homemade vinegar should not be used for preserving, where safety requires a minimum 5 percent acidity. Homemade vinegar is also difficult to protect from contaminants in the air that can produce unpleasant flavors or ruin the process altogether.

EVERYBODY HAS A MOTHER The mother of the vinegar is the gelatinous film or mat, thick or thin, that grows across the top of fermenting vinegar. It is made almost completely of acetic bacteria and some form of it is essential for the successful production of vinegar. Frequently, and particularly if disturbed, the mother will sink to the bottom of the barrel, vat, or bottle and, contrary to popular belief, die. Without oxygen, the thin mat of bacteria and cellulose cannot survive and begins to decay, unpleasantly influencing the taste of the vinegar. The mother can also bog down commercial production by clogging machinery, and commercial producers work to develop vinegars with a minimal tendency to form a mother.

If you want to try your hand at making vinegar, the guidelines set down by the United States Department of Agriculture (USDA) in 1924 have not been improved upon. For more detailed information, including advice for trouble-shooting the many problems that can arise in home vinegar making, I recommend L. J. Diggs's book *Vinegar*. Mr. Diggs offers considerable detail about the process recommended by the USDA that the vinegar-obsessed home producer will find interesting and helpful.

The Official Home Vinegar Production Guidelines,
University of California, 1924

When you begin, make certain that all of your equipment, your workspace, your utensils, your hands, and your clothes are absolutely clean. The vinegar itself should never come in contact with metal. Use cheesecloth, paper, or plastic to strain the liquid. When bottled, use corks to close rather than metal screw tops.

Fill a four-gallon stone or glass jar about two-thirds full of unpasteurized grape juice or the juice of crushed fruit such as grapes, apples, pineapple, or pears. Mix a cake of compressed yeast with a small amount of the juice and add it to the jar. Cover with several layers of cheesecloth to keep out dust, insects, and other contaminants in the air. Keep the jar in an easily accessible, warm, dark area. Stir it daily, breaking up any surface crust formation. This will help prevent mold and insure a complete fermentation. This process will take about six days.

Strain the fermented liquid through cheesecloth and return it to the jar. Inoculate with a good vinegar, using one quarter the amount of the juice. Cover with cheesecloth and let the mixture sit in a dark, warm place until the alcohol has been converted to acetic acid. Depending on the room temperature, this process can take from a few weeks to a few months. For informal vinegar making, it is not necessary to test for acid content. Rely upon your palate to tell you when your vinegar is complete.

When you are satisfied with the taste of your homemade vinegar, you should strain it through a paper coffee filter and bottle it. Used wine bottles, especially the small bottles, are perfect for storing homemade vinegars. Be sure to close with a cork.

The bacteria in the vinegar may continue their activity after filtering and bottling. For this reason, you may wish to heat your vinegar to 160 degrees F. to kill the vinegar culture. This informal pasteurization will discourage the formation of a mother, though [the vinegar] should be bottled before it cools significantly to decrease the possibility of contamination with fresh acetobacters. Do not heat the vinegar past 160 degrees F., or the acetic acid will begin to evaporate and there will be a loss of strength, aroma, and flavor.

If you would prefer to begin with a substrate that is already fermented, red wine will yield better results than white wine. White wine contains considerable sulfur dioxide, which inhibits the growth of the essential acetobacters.

LEVELS OF ACIDITY

Acidity or grain refers to the percentage of acetic acid in a particular vinegar. For nearly all vinegars the acidity is noted on the label, as a percentage (for example, 6 percent) or in terms of grain (for example, 60 grain). The higher the percentage or grain, the stronger the vinegar. For preserving, a minimum acidity level of 5 percent is required. Except for preserving, taste is the primary consideration when choosing a vinegar. The stronger the acidity, the more it dominates the taste, frequently eclipsing the flavors of the substrate. For this reason, consideration should be given to acidity when choosing vinegars for culinary purposes.

In general, recipes do not indicate the optimum acidity of the vinegar required. Rarely is acidity even mentioned, even though it is one of the most important aspects of the vinegar you choose. With levels ranging from 4.5 (or lower if you consider some of the oriental varieties) to 9.0 percent, acidity plays an important role in shaping the outcome of your recipe. This became very clear to me when I was working on my first cookbook and received a phone call from one of the editors who had just made my Raspberry Hollandaise. It was good, she said, but overly tart; might I consider reducing the level of vinegar? Checking the label, I discovered that I had been making the sauce for years with a low-acid, 4.5 percent raspberry vinegar; she had used a 7.5 percent version. Not only would her hollandaise have been much harsher and more acidic, but also the aroma and the voluptuousness of the raspberry flavor, which the vinegar was intended to impart, would have been eclipsed. Since then, I always indicate the recommended acidic level for a particular dish.

THE VINEGAR MAN Lawrence Diggs claims the name of The Vinegar Man. His exuberance for the acidic liquid, an enthusiasm that led him into four years of research on the topic, makes it a fitting title. In 1989, he self-published a book, Vinegar: The User-Friendly Standard Text, Reference, and Guide to Appreciating, Making, and Enjoying Vinegar, that is an exhaustive account of vinegar and its making throughout history.

Diggs is a Soto Zen Buddhist. Seeking information on vinegar production as a way to support a monastic retreat he hoped to build, Diggs became an expert on the subject. Full of strange historical and legal facts, names for vinegar in thirty languages, instructions for home production, and recipes, Vinegar may be the only cookbook in the world with its own theme song. The lyrics to Diggs's song, "The Vinegar Man," are included. The book's lack of standard production values is eclipsed by the author's unfettered enthusiasm for his subject.

> Here comes the vinegar man
> To help all his vinegar fans
> Here comes the vinegar man
> To make this a vinegar land
> It's the man of the hour
> With his great sour power
> In his vinegar dressings
> He brings us great blessings
> L. J. Diggs, "The Vinegar Man"

FLAVORED VINEGARS

Making your own vinegar can be an unpredictable process, but it is easy and sensible to flavor vinegars yourself. As anyone who has ever scanned a gourmet market shelf knows, specialty vinegars can be absurdly expensive. As with flavored oils, many of the producers are really more accurately described as bottlers who buy commercial vinegar in bulk—often the same types that are available to you—bottle it, add a few sprigs of basil or a clove of garlic on a stick, and charge a huge price for their minimal effort. Even some of the better versions on the market are diluted with distilled vinegar, which I find adds an unpleasant sharpness.

In a proliferation of magazine articles and chapters in cookbooks the home cook can acquire information on making flavored vinegars. The instructions vary as widely as do the recommendations for seasonings and flavorings. Some instruct you to heat or even boil the vinegar, either before you pour it over the flavoring agents or together with the flavoring agents. Some tell you to add, say, the raspberries, and then allow the vinegar mixture to sit in a dark place for anywhere from a day to a month or, in one case, a year. Some insist that you strain the vinegar immediately after combining it with the flavorings. Others call for the addition of sugar or honey. While most recommend that you store your flavored vinegars in a dark place, occasionally you will be instructed to place the bottles on a sunny windowsill. The afternoon sun may make the bottles shimmer like so many bright kitchen jewels, but it will also damage the delicate flavor of the vinegars. The specific techniques I recommend in this book (see pages 144–153) have given me the best, most consistent results.

Among flavored vinegars, raspberry vinegar is probably the oldest, most common, and most readily available. Excellent brands abound in the marketplace and are available to the average cook without much of a chase to find them. Blueberry vinegar is also fairly common and quite delicious. I use raspberry vinegar often in my cooking. When I want a strong berry flavor, I prefer a low-acid variety and one made with black rather than red raspberries: They have a richer, more voluptuous flavor. Raspberry vinegars are produced by several domestic companies and are imported from France. Kozlowski Farms in Sonoma County, California, produces outstanding low-acid berry vinegars, both red and black, and a very good blueberry vinegar, too. If you are seeking one with a higher acid content, I recommend a French vinegar. Le Vinaigre and Velux both make particularly good versions with enough raspberry flavor to stand up to the higher acid level. If you find a vinegar with good flavor but a level of acidity too sharp for your palate, the addition of a small amount of wine will mellow it.

There is one excellent reason to make your own berry vinegar: a berry patch that produces more than you can eat. Raspberries and blueberries are expensive, and with all of the excellent raspberry vinegars available commercially, it is generally much less costly to buy a version you like than to make one, unless you can make it with your own berries. If you are lucky enough to live in an agricultural area, you might be able to buy flats of berries cheaply enough to make a batch of vinegar each year. It is worth the effort to make your own if you can do it reasonably inexpensively, but it is also comforting to know that there are many good commercial versions available.

VINEGAR TASTING

Vinegar tasting might strike the novice as a strange thing to do. After all, vinegar, unlike wine, is not something we drink for pleasure or for quenching thirst. But what other way is there to find vinegars you like except to taste and compare them? There are no texts for tasting vinegars, no accepted standard of judging, and no single standard method of tasting. We are pretty much on our own, but it is not difficult to learn the characteristics of a good vinegar and to learn to recognize them.

I have tasted vinegars formally, high up in the Italian hill town of Volpaia, for example, where the American writer John Meis arranged a special preview of the flavored vinegars made at Castello di Volpaia. Seven different vinegars were poured from fresh bottles into seven wineglasses, and we sipped and compared and refreshed our palates with bottled spring water. We tried to identify the different components that contributed to the complex blends known as *erbe, spezie, orto, fiori,* and *fresco.* The highlight of the tasting was, for me anyway, when our guide took us to the tiny production facility a few kilometers away and opened the spigot on one of the aging and flavoring tanks. The *orto*—or vegetable garden—vinegar was about four months into its aging process and, much to my delight, one sip revealed that the first flavor to develop was garlic. It was a joy on the palate, and the finished product was delicious, too, if somewhat mellower and more balanced than that first powerhouse taste. I have also tasted vinegars informally, licked from the palm of my hand where a friend has poured the sample of a personal favorite. It is not nearly so strange as it sounds.

What to look for in vinegar is very much what to look for in wine. It should be pleasing to the eye, with clearness and clarity. The aroma should be clean—if it is very strong, you will detect that immediately because your head will go back. We react to the scent of acetic acid, just as we do to the scent of alcohol. There should be no hint of decay. In general, vinegars never smell like the grape varieties they are made from, with the exception of Pinot Noir and Muscat, which have a high residual fragrance. The vinegar should taste pleasing and full, not just acidic, and it should have body, depth of flavor, and character. Consider the aftertaste. Is it pleasant? Does it linger?

When tasting for comparison, choose vinegars of a similar type. For example, taste a selection of unflavored red wine vinegars in a range of acidic levels. Taste and compare several raspberry vinegars, judging them for their bouquet and fruitiness. It makes little sense to taste a variety of vinegars with unrelated qualities, unless you merely want to become acquainted with their flavors.

Vinegar may be tasted straight, diluted, and on sugar cubes. To taste a vinegar straight, you simply pour a small quantity into a glass—a wineglass works perfectly. After looking at it in the light and smelling it, take a small sip, holding it in your mouth for a few seconds and swallowing it slowly. Before tasting the next vinegar, cleanse and relax your palate with a drink of unflavored mineral water and a small piece of celery or bread. Repeat the process until you have tasted all your vinegars. This method allows you to taste the vinegar directly at its full intensity, but it is hard on the palate and difficult to keep your taste buds open during the assault of so much acetic acid. I do not recommend your tasting more than five or six vinegars by this method at one seating.

A method that is easier on the palate is to dilute one teaspoon of vinegar with two tablespoons of good bottled water. Your palate does not wear out so quickly, nor do you get the full intensity of the flavor. This is a good method if for some reason you find yourself needing to taste many vinegars.

A third method is dramatic and at least one expert on vinegar, Dante Bagnani, considers it purely for show. Others recommend it, and I think it is a good idea when a large group is tasting. It uses fewer glasses and less vinegar and the palate does seem to stay active. To taste with sugar cubes, place the vinegars to be tasted in wineglasses with good-size openings. Most sugar cubes are made to dissolve quickly; you should use Domino cubes for vinegar tasting. Each taster dips a sugar cube quickly into the vinegar and then sucks the vinegar out of it. There is a hint of sweetness but not an overwhelming amount, and the taste buds generally stay perky through eight or nine samples. A fresh sugar cube should be used for each vinegar.

MENU FOR A VINEGAR TASTING

For each taster provide:
1 Domino sugar cube for each vinegar that will be tasted, large glass of water, several saltines or breadsticks, an evaluation sheet (see page 247) and pencil, and a napkin.

On the common table place:
Bottles of vinegars to be tasted; eight-ounce wineglasses
filled with between one and two inches of the vinegars, the
glasses being arranged in front of their corresponding bot-
tles, and pitchers of water.

COOKING WITH VINEGAR

Sometimes vinegar is the centerpiece of a recipe, in a sparkling vinaigrette, perhaps, or a *mignonette* sauce. Its distinctive qualities give the dish its character and shape. All
sorts of pickled fruits and vegetables, condiments as diverse
as ketchup, prepared mustards, Tabasco sauce, chutneys,
and salsas rely on vinegar for their nuances of tartness and
pleasant sourness. Sometimes vinegar is, however, a deeper
component, a supporting player brought in early in the
show, perhaps in a marinade or as one of many elements
in a sauce, such as in Chicken *au Vinaigre* (page 130). Its
touch then is more subtle, indirect, and its acidity and
particular flavor help to shape the building blocks of a
dish. It may not be distinctly recognizable in the final product, but its contribution is nonetheless essential to the outcome.

When using vinegar in a marinade, you must understand its function. Acids denature, or cook protein. When
you submerge a piece of protein, a chicken breast, let us say,
into pure vinegar, the acetic acid goes to work immediately
on the cellular structure of the protein. Your chicken will be
"cooked," that is, the protein will be denatured, and it will
be dry and have an unpleasant texture. This is obviously

not the result you want. In marinating any cut of meat or poultry, you should use a combination of oil, acid, spices, and herbs.

USES FOR VINEGAR

TYPE OF VINEGAR	PRICE RANGE	RECOMMENDED USES
BALSAMIC	Inexpensive to expensive	Sauces, dressings, marinades, condiment
BALSAMIC, TRADITIONAL	Extremely expensive	Condiment
BLACK	Inexpensive	Flavoring, Chinese and other Pacific Rim cuisines
CANE	Inexpensive	Philippine cuisine
CHAMPAGNE	Moderate	Fruit vinegars, light dressings
CIDER	Inexpensive to moderate	Preserves and chutneys
DISTILLED (white)	Inexpensive	Cleaning and general household uses
MALT	Inexpensive to moderate	Pickling, ketchup, fish and chips
PINEAPPLE	Moderate	Dressings, salsas, flavoring
RASPBERRY	Moderate to expensive	Dressings, marinades, emulsions, flavoring, condiment
RED WINE	Moderate	Hearty dressings, sauces, marinades, spice vinegars
RICE	Inexpensive to moderate	Thai and Japanese cuisine, with oysters, seafood
SHERRY	Moderate to expensive	Sauces, soups, dressings
WHITE WINE	Moderate	Dressings, emulsions, herb vinegars, fruit vinegars

With beef, pork, and lamb, a vinegar marinade denatures only the surface of the meat and is not particularly effective at tenderizing it. The only really effective way of tenderizing meat is mechanical. A vinegar solution will penetrate somewhat deeper if the cut has been pricked with a fork, but this also causes a loss of fluids when it is cooked. For flavoring larger cuts of meat such as a beef tenderloin or a leg of lamb, a dry marinade such as a mixture of finely chopped parsley or rosemary, lemon zest, and garlic works best. Liquid oil and vinegar marinades are excellent for flavoring cubed or thinly sliced meats for stews, curries, or various sorts of kabobs.

Because the action of vinegar on certain proteins works counter to what we want, we must be careful not to let its denaturing action go too far. Vinegar does prevent overcooking—or the coagulation of the protein—in emulsified sauces made with eggs. It can save us before we have gone too far. Coagulation is the one problem in an emulsified sauce that cannot be corrected. A sauce can break—that is, the oil can precipitate out of the emulsion—and be repaired, but chunks of cooked and coagulated egg protein will never become uncoagulated. Harold McGee cites a study in his book *On Food and Cooking* that demonstrates the principle: In emulsified sauces with a neutral pH, the egg protein curdled at temperatures between 160 degrees and 175 degrees F. The addition of vinegar allowed the sauces to be heated up to 195 degrees F. Under normal conditions, sauces are made at temperatures below 160 degrees F., the temperature at which the butter begins to separate out from the emulsion. But every cook looks away for a moment, gets distracted, or lets the heat rise too high on occasion, and it is helpful to have this knowledge as insurance. A cook whose warm emulsions curdle would do well to get into the habit of adding a teaspoon of a compatible vinegar before beginning.

BALSAMIC VINEGAR AND THE ALCHEMY OF TIME

> In Modena, in the attics of ancient buildings, they have been making a vinegar for centuries. A vinegar, or rather a liqueur, which demands an entire life from those who make it.
>
> Vincenzo Buonassisi, from a *Consortium of Producers of the Traditional Balsamic Vinegar of Modena* pamphlet, 1988.

> It's something capable of raising the dead.
>
> Luigi Mani, from the above pamphlet.

Aceto balsamico is to vinegar what extra virgin olive oil is to oil: It is provocative, inspiring, diverse, and delicious beyond its traditional functions. Balsamic vinegar stands alone in the culinary world as a rich, dark, luscious substance that has a taste, a history, a process of production, and a price that set it apart from any other vinegar. *Aceto balsamico* is produced solely in one small region of northern Italy, but that geographical limitation is the only variable that is not challenged when enthusiasts discuss their favorite versions. Balsamic vinegar—its production and aging, its taste, its judging, its marketing—evokes the same pride and fervor as do the olive oils from the Mediterranean's prime olive-growing regions.

If you have picked up a bottle from your grocer's shelf recently, paying a modest price most likely under ten dollars, you might wonder what all the fuss is about. Certainly it has a wonderful flavor—some brands even seem to be so rich as to be drinkable—but it is difficult to imagine offering large sums of money for another taste. So, whence this mystique, these exotic claims? First of all, few people outside the region of production have tasted the true balsamic vinegar. Most of what is brought to this country is an officially sanctioned substitute. The supply of the true vinegar cannot keep up with the demand. Production remains the very slow, laborious process it has been for centuries, and to change it would be to change the very nature of the vinegar itself, thus creating something other than true, or traditional, *aceto balsamico*.

The Emilia-Romagna region of Italy is bordered by the Venezia-Euganea and Lombardy regions to the north, the Adriatic Sea to the east, Liguria to the southwest, and Tuscany and The Marches to the south. Emilia-Romagna spans nearly the whole width of the peninsula, stretching from the Adriatic Sea to within a few miles of the Gulf of Genoa. It is to the heart of this northern Italian region that we must turn to discover the true *aceto balsamico tradizionale*, the secret treasure of Modena and Emilia.

It appears that the vinegar was produced as early as the eleventh century, when records show that Duke Boniface of Canossa presented a barrel of it as a coronation gift to the Holy Roman emperor, Henry III, in 1046. The great ducal family of the region, the Estes, served it as a cordial and gave it as gifts to the important statesmen of Europe. It was also used as a tonic for protection against the plague. After the decline of the Este family, the vinegar was rarely sent away and production gradually diminished. It remained prized in regional households, a well-kept Modenese secret, and it was not until the late 1970s that signs of a revival appeared and imitators proliferated. Even as the reputation of the foods of the region grew—prosciutto and Parmesan cheese, for example—*aceto balsamico* remained in relative obscurity until recently.

True balsamic vinegar is so valued because of its exquisite aromas and the flavors that develop while it is aging, differences so distinct, so singular, that they defy comparison with other vinegars. It is always sweet and always a little sour, but the intensity of each varies greatly. Preferences vary throughout the region of production and it is not uncommon to find passionate arguments between afficionados in Modena, who prefer the drier version produced there, and afficionados in Emilia who claim that their sweeter versions are superior.

The character of the vinegar is achieved through wood aging and a labyrinthine process that would thwart any but the most dedicated. The white Trebbiano grape is the most commonly used, although Malvasia, Occhio di Gatto, Spergola, and the more common red Lambrusco have all released their juices to become *aceto balsamico*. After the grapes are crushed and the stems removed, the resulting must—the unfermented juice of pressed grapes—sits until the first signs of fermentation. It is then filtered and the liquid is simmered in copper caldrons over wood fires until reduced by 40 percent. The liquid is placed in demijohns or small stainless steel vats and, come spring, the juice is inoculated with an old vinegar and begins the first of a series of multiple transfers to progressively smaller wooden barrels, the *batteria*. As summer approaches and the temperature of the reduced liquid begins to rise, two processes occur nearly simultaneously: alcoholic fermentation occurs as yeast turns the sugar to alcohol, and acetic oxidation takes place as acetobacters change the alcohol to acetic acid.

As historical records as early as the thirteenth century document, this process traditionally takes place in the attic, where temperatures fluctuate with the extremes of the season. The intensity of the heat of a summer day, at which time the chemical activity is at its peak, and the near freezing nights of winter when the chemical activity is still are both essential for the slow processing of the vinegar. Interestingly, women made most of the *aceto balsamico*. The *batteria* was often a part of the dowry, and art works dating from the thirteenth century depict women in their attics among the wooden casks. A *batteria* is dated and vinegars produced from a particular *batteria* bear that date. Thus, when you see an *aceto balsamico tradizionale* dated 1650, that date refers to the beginning of the particular *batteria* that produced the vinegar. The older the *batteria* the more precious, and thus the more expensive, is the vinegar.

The liquid is shifted, generally once a year, through the range of seasoned casks of diminishing sizes. Oak and chestnut are the most common woods, though cherry, locust, ash, alder, mulberry, and juniper are used as well, each variety of wood making its imprint on the final flavor. With an evaporation rate of 10 percent a year, a hundred liters of must become, twelve years later, a mere fifteen liters of vinegar. Most often further aging and, hence, further evaporation, is required. We begin to understand the high retail cost.

In response to the phenomenal new interest in balsamic vinegar, and the predictable surge of imitators, the Italian government has bestowed its recognition and blessing upon the dark, rich liquid by offering an official designation for vinegars of a certain quality. *Denominazione di origine controllata (DOC)*, parallel to the French *appellation controlée*, recognizes the geographical areas and methods of production and aging in a way previously offered only to wines. For a vinegar to qualify it must be from Modena or neighboring Reggio nell'Emilia. It must be made not from wine but from cooked grape must according to the traditional method. Absolutely no flavorings or other ingredients can be added and the vinegar must be aged for a minimum of twelve years.

The licensing of the special vinegar is controlled by the Consortium of Producers of the Traditional Balsamic Vinegar of Modena. To receive the government sanction of *DOC*, the vinegar must be submitted to the official board of tasters for approval. About one third of the vinegars submitted each year receive the designation, and generally those approved are between twenty and thirty years old. The twelve-year-old vinegars are thought to be too young and immature in flavor.

With the introduction of the *DOC* designation came officially required packaging as well. The amount of approved vinegar that a producer wishes to sell is delivered in bulk to the consortium, where it is bottled in specially designed, 100-cc bottles and closed with the consortium's official wax seal. It is then returned to the producer, who labels it, always including the required *"aceto balsamico tradizionale di Modena"* designation and the date of the *batteria*. The bottles come in two shapes, one with the vinegar from Reggio nell'Emilia, the other holding the Modenese vinegar.

Like the very best olive oils, traditional balsamic vinegar is more of a condiment than a cooking agent. The very oldest and finest is reserved for drinking or for flavoring well-aged wine vinegar. The use of traditional balsamic vinegar as an elixir is not as common as it once was, although a splash in cocktails and other iced drinks is still considered delicious and refreshing. Many think even that is a waste, so precious has the concoction become.

If the dark liquid is used on salad, it is in companionship with olive oil and other vinegar. It may be added to mayonnaise for flavor. In cream and butter sauces for both vegetables and seafood, especially for steamed mollusks and crustaceans, a splash of an old, true balsamic vinegar magically transforms the dish. An extravagant cook may add a liberal splash to tomato sauces and meat ragouts to intensify their flavors, and Parmesan cheese melted with white truffle shavings is said to be heavenly when sprinkled with the vinegar.

The government's aim when it offered the *DOC* designation to the vinegar was to distinguish the true *aceto balsamic tradizionale* from the imitators that have flourished. As knowledge of *aceto balsamico* has spread beyond its native Modena, demand has soared and the decline in production has slowly begun to reverse. Still, because of the aging required, there is not enough to satisfy the demand. Thus, we find an aged wine vinegar that has been fortified with caramelized sugar, herbs, and other flavorings legally described as Aceto Balsamico di Modena. Detractors call it *aceto industriale*, but this pleasant vinegar has given most of the outside world its first taste of "balsamic vinegar," and still constitutes much of what is available and affordable in this country today. Four brands are imported from Italy, although they are bottled and sold under a variety of specialty labels. The key distinction between these vinegars and traditional balsamic vinegar is the term *"tradizionale."* Although similar labeling restrictions do not apply in the United States, it is easy to distinguish the authentic substance. Disregard all of the claims and confusion, ignore all the labels that scream at us from the grocer's shelves. It is really quite simple to determine if you are holding the real thing in your hands. First, it must be in one of the two types of approved glass bottles and have the consortium's seal. Anything sold in quantities over 100 cc, or 3.3 ounces, is fraudulent. Second, true *aceto balsamico* is extremely viscous, a dark brown liquid that coats the neck of the jar when turned on its side. When righted, it slowly oozes down the glass, all thick and syrupy and voluptuous. The contents of a bottle of vinegar that has been turned and then righted that splash happily back into place will not be the traditional vinegar of Modena. You can also recognize the authentic by its price; it is exorbitantly expensive, selling for well over a hundred dollars even for the younger versions.

Like cheese and wine, *aceto balsamico* is said to reflect the character of its maker. "Violent people make violent vinegar; sweet old people make sweet old vinegar," claims Glauco Smadelli, a producer, a taster, and a family doctor, who added, "and it might even be said, though more so in the past than now, that noble people make noble vinegar because they had the best of materials to work with."

> Modena's vinegar is the result of the alchemy of time. Thus when you taste an ancient balsamic vinegar you have the immediate pleasure of the taste but you also receive a revelation of the magic that lies in the sequence of toppings up and the dedicated attention of the craftsman. You will detect all this in a thousand and one shadings of flavor and your enjoyment of them and appreciation will make you part of the art and wisdom of those who have preceded us down the years.
>
> Renato Bergonzini, from a *Consortium of Producers of the Traditional Balsamic Vinegar of Modena* pamphlet, 1988

PART THREE

The Annotated Oil & Vinegar Pantry

TODAY WE HAVE SUCH VARIED LIFESTYLES THAT no common formula can address all of our culinary and nutritional needs. In the 1950s when the two-parent family was the American norm, everyone ate at home, Mom cooked, and on occasion, the family visited a restaurant together. That common fabric has frayed and people tend to their nutritional needs in all manner of ways from the familiar and traditional to the strange and bizarre. Some families still eat nearly every meal together, the meals are cooked from scratch from well-stocked cupboards and refrigerators, and Mom is still at the helm. But nowadays many people rarely or never cook, relying instead on a plethora of fast-food restaurants and gourmet take-out delicatessens. Others nourish themselves on the prepared foods offered for sale in grocery stores, eating dishes that need no more attention than the opening of a package and the turning of a dial on a microwave oven. Our pantries look very different from those of our mothers and grandmothers.

Even with today's diverse eating styles and the great number of people who never cook, we have more culinary options than we did when Mrs. Cleaver opened her cupboard to prepare dinner for Ward, Wally, and the Beaver. Angelo Pellegrini, in his book *The Unprejudiced Palate*, tells a revealing story—written in the 1940s—of cooking at a college friend's house and requesting olive oil to douse the rabbit he was preparing. None was to be found in the pantry, but there was some in the medicine cabinet, kept there by his friend's mother and used to rub on her scalp. How far we have come. We may not cook as regularly as Mrs. Cleaver did, but our culinary horizons have broadened immensely and deliciously.

Whether we cook frequently or out of rare desperation, it is a good idea to have a well-planned and well-stocked pantry available when the need or impulse strikes us. Certain items—a selection of dried pastas, for example, canned chicken broth, Tabasco sauce—make it simple to put a meal together on short notice. The proper selection of oils and vinegars makes the process even easier and our spur-of-the-moment repertoire more diverse.

When stocking your oil and vinegar pantry, assess your cooking habits realistically and purchase quantities that reflect them. Do not buy olive oil by the gallon or even by the liter if you will use it only three or four times a year. Likewise, do not buy six-ounce bottles of your favorite oil or vinegar if you use it up in a week or even a month. For both oils and vinegars, purchase sizes that you will use within six months. Many oils and vinegars will keep longer than that, of course, but the flavor of most products will begin to deteriorate after a few months on the shelf.

THE WELL-STOCKED PANTRY For the culinary enthusiast, a well-stocked pantry will have a generous and interesting selection of oils and vinegars. In mine, I would include the following.

OILS
General purpose (refined): *Peanut, corn, safflower, and pure olive oil*
Nut: *Hazelnut, walnut; store in the refrigerator*
Specialty oils: *Extra virgin olive oil of several varieties, such as general, robust green (Tuscan), light golden (French or Italian Riviera); toasted sesame*
Unrefined oils *of choice, especially corn*
Flavored oils: *Extra virgin olive oil with hot peppers, truffle oil, vanilla oil*

VINEGARS
General purpose: *Distilled, apple cider, red wine (6–6.5 percent acidity), white wine (6–6.5 percent acidity), raspberry (6–7 percent acidity), sherry (6–7 percent acidity)*
Specialty: *Low-acid raspberry (up to 5 percent acidity), rice (unseasoned; under 5 percent acidity), cranberry (homemade, up to 6.5 percent acidity), low-acid blueberry, floral, balsamic vinegar*
Other: *Flavored varieties that you use frequently*

THE NOT-QUITE-BARE CUPBOARD For the reluctant cook, the essentials are fewer, but you never know when an emergency may arise, and if you keep these items on hand, you'll usually be able to handle it with ease and comfort. You might even be inspired to try your hand at a few recipes.

OILS
1 general-purpose oil: pure olive oil, corn oil, or peanut oil
1 good-tasting extra virgin olive oil
1 small bottle of extra virgin olive oil with hot peppers (for pizza)

VINEGAR
1 small bottle red wine vinegar, 6–6.5 percent acidity
1 small bottle champagne vinegar, 6–7 percent acidity
1 small bottle raspberry vinegar, 4.5 percent acidity

OILS

ALMOND OIL A mildly flavored oil high in monounsaturated fats, low in saturated fats, with a high smoke point. Almond oil, like almonds, is, however, expensive, and the oil is not widely used for general cooking.

AVOCADO OIL A delicate, nutty-flavored oil pressed directly from the fruit of the avocado. It has a high smoke point and is rich in monounsaturated fatty acids, but limited production, almost exclusively in California, keeps it relatively expensive.

CANOLA (RAPESEED) OIL The flavorless oil from the rapeseed is praised for its low percentage of saturated fat. It was widely used in Europe, though its popularity declined during the 1940s, probably because it contains erucic acid, which can cause liver damage. New species of the plant have resulted in a recent dramatic increase in production in Europe. The Canadian variety has had most of the acid bred out of the plants, though it is still present in trace amounts. Rapeseed oil is widely used in vegetable oil blends.

COCONUT OIL The highly saturated oil from the coconut palm is not widely used as a domestic cooking oil. It is, however, used extensively in commercial production of cooking oil blends and margarines.

CORN OIL The widely used oil of the corn kernel. Its high smoke point, mild taste, and high percentage of polyunsaturated fatty acids makes refined corn oil one of the most popular of the commercial oils. In its unrefined form, it is rich tasting, with a flavor evocative of fresh popcorn.

COTTONSEED OIL The by-product of cotton production, cottonseed oil has been widely used in commercial food production primarily because it is cheap. It is also high in saturated fats and contains residual pesticides in substantial quantities.

FLAXSEED OIL A relatively new oil marketed as a food supplement rather than a cooking oil; high in two essential fatty acids, linoleic acid and alphalinolenic acid. This highly unstable oil must be stored in a cool, dark place and used within a few months of being processed.

GRAPESEED OIL The oil from the grape seed has been heralded for its high percentage of polyunsaturated fatty acids—77 percent according to some studies—but with research indicating the superiority of monounsaturated fats, grapeseed oil has not seen the surge of popularity that was once predicted. It is a very mild oil with a high smoke point, but its benefits do not override its higher price.

HAZELNUT OIL A highly unstable, therefore perishable, oil full of the rich flavor of the nut. The delicate taste is destroyed by heat, so this oil is best used for dressings and uncooked sauces. It must be refrigerated.

LINSEED OIL A highly refined oil pressed from flax seeds. It oxidizes rapidly and is generally considered inedible, although it was sold regularly in health food stores until recently because of its reputed health benefits; it has been replaced by unrefined flaxseed oil.

MUSTARD OIL An inexpensive oil generally found only in specialty shops that sell international products. Widely used only in India, it is also used in some commercial food production in spite of the fact that it contains a large quantity of erucic acid. It is high in monounsaturates and has a mild yet distinctive flavor with a flash of heat in the taste.

OLIVE OIL, EXTRA VIRGIN The most flavorful of the olive oils; major commercial brands are generally a blend of refined olive oil with a percentage of unrefined olive oil added to produce the robust flavor and deeper color. True extra virgin oils, consisting entirely of unrefined oil from the first pressing, are produced on small farms, are expensive, and are the best-tasting olive oils.

OLIVE OIL, LITE Pure, refined olive oil with little or none of the characteristic taste or color of olives; acceptable for deep-frying.

OLIVE OIL, PURE 100 percent olive oil that has been refined. It has more color and more olive taste than does "lite" olive oil. A good oil for general cooking when more delicate flavors are not required or will be destroyed by high heat.

PALM OIL Inexpensive and tasteless, the oil of both the fruit and the kernel are used throughout the world in commercial food production and general cooking, in spite of the fact that the oil is highly saturated.

PEANUT OIL Sold almost exclusively in its refined state, peanut oil is an extremely popular cooking oil. It retains some natural flavor, adding a pleasant taste to many recipes, though not so much as to interfere with other ingredients.

PUMPKIN SEED OIL A dark and richly flavorful oil that is both highly unstable and very hard to find. It has a low smoke point and its taste is destroyed by heat, thus making it appropriate for salads and cold sauces.

RICE BRAN OIL A refined oil common in Japan but expensive and hard to find in the United States; heralded briefly as the new "healthy" oil, it has a fatty acid profile that makes it inferior to less expensive, better-tasting oils.

SAFFLOWER OIL An oil prized for its high percentage of polyunsaturates and monounsaturates. It is light in color and tasteless, making it a good all-purpose cooking oil.

SESAME OIL Probably the first oil ever used, sesame oil today is best known for its flavorful contribution to oriental cuisine.

SESAME OIL, TOASTED One of the key flavoring agents of many Asian cuisines. It has a rich, dominant flavor. Good for flavoring stir-fried meats and vegetables.

SOY OIL A flavorless oil with a fatty acid profile that does not make it particularly attractive for culinary uses. It is often hydrogenated and used in commercial food preparation. Because it foams at higher temperatures, it is not recommended for deep-frying.

SUNFLOWER OIL One of the most common domestic cooking oils worldwide, sunflower oil is high in polyunsaturated fats. It is also used extensively in commercial production.

WALNUT OIL A delicate, fragrant oil pressed from toasted walnuts. European brands currently offer the best-tasting walnut oils. Highly unstable; should be refrigerated.

VINEGARS

BALSAMIC VINEGAR An aged wine vinegar from Modena, Italy, that has been fortified with caramelized sugar, herbs, and other flavorings; developed to satisfy the demand for traditional balsamic vinegar, which is rare and costly.

BALSAMIC VINEGAR, TRADITIONAL A rare vinegar made from the cooked juice of grapes and aged for a minimum of twelve years in a series of wooden casks known as a *batteria*; must be approved by the Italian government and sold in specially designed bottles in order to bear the seal and designation *"aceto balsamico tradizionale"*; extremely expensive.

BLACK VINEGAR A very low acid vinegar (2.5 percent) that is blended with rice, sugar, and spices to achieve its characteristic flavor; used primarily in Pacific Rim cuisines.

CANE VINEGAR Fermented from sugar cane extract and water, this low-acid vinegar is common in the cuisine of the Philippines.

CHAMPAGNE VINEGAR Made from fermented champagne grapes; frequently a very sharp wine vinegar, though the best are mellow and delicate. Use in sauces for lighter poultry and seafood. Good for fruit- and herb-flavored vinegars. Its flavor tends not to compete with other ingredients.

CIDER VINEGAR Made from apples and essential for making most chutneys; sprinkled on French fries in Canada; good in pies and pie crusts.

DISTILLED OR SPIRIT VINEGAR Called for in certain pickling recipes; excellent for cleaning; this is the vinegar used in most commercial food products.

MALT VINEGAR Once made from beer and now made from a sugar infusion of cereal starches, its claim to fame is as a condiment for fish and chips, especially in England; good for pickling, and for making ketchup and chutney; the vinegar of choice in Great Britain.

PINEAPPLE VINEGAR A common and flavorful vinegar used widely in Mexico. Diana Kennedy, the noted food writer, mentions it in her texts on the foods of Mexico and provides instructions for making it.

RASPBERRY VINEGAR, HIGH-ACID White wine or red wine vinegar that has been flavored with raspberries or, more commonly, raspberry syrup. Certain imported brands produce versions that retain a great deal of raspberry flavor after cooking, which makes them excellent for marinades, sauces, and warm vinaigrettes.

RASPBERRY VINEGAR, LOW-ACID Produced in the same manner as the high-acid versions, but this vinegar is preferable for sauces in which the flavor of raspberries is to be highlighted; use in mayonnaise, hollandaise, marinades for vegetables.

RED WINE VINEGAR Made from red wine; can offer a rich depth of flavor; excellent for meat marinades and sauces, and in vinaigrettes for robust salads.

RICE VINEGAR, SEASONED The sweetened version of this oriental vinegar made from rice has limited use. Depending on the brand, the sweetness can be overbearing, and the other flavorings frequently contribute a chemical taste.

RICE VINEGAR, UNSEASONED An evocative, subtle sweetness informs the vinegar of the Orient, and it is a natural component of many Asian dishes. Its flavor is common at *sushi* bars, where it is used to make the pickled ginger that is invariably served as a condiment and as a dressing on the sliced cucumbers known as *sunumono*, after *su*, the name of the vinegar in Japanese.

SHERRY VINEGAR Produced in Spain from sherry wine, this vinegar is flavorful and distinctive. It is aged in wooden casks and blends well with olive oil, walnut and hazelnut oils, slightly sweet dishes, and smoked poultry salads.

WHITE WINE VINEGAR Made from white wine, this vinegar can be sharp or mellow, depending on the original substrate. Essential for certain light vinaigrettes, *beurre blanc*, and marinades for light meats and seafood.

PART FOUR

An Oil & Vinegar Cookbook

COOKING WITH SPECIALTY OILS

DECIDING WHICH RECIPES TO INCLUDE IN this section and which to banish was not an easy task. I cook with oil all the time, but I wanted this section to highlight aspects of the oils featured, not just include them as one of many minor players. Frequently, the best way to feature the special taste of an oil is with little or no cooking, and several of those methods are described in the Little Recipes that begin this section. Most of the remaining recipes attempt to demonstrate the ways in which the character of a certain oil can be the focus, the point, of the dish. The white bean soup on page 95 is lovely, but it is sublime with just the right oil drizzled over it. Of course, I could not resist including some special favorites—Garden Minestrone, for example—that do not feature an oil as a primary focus, but depend upon its good quality for success.

If you are new to the world of specialty oils, you are in for a very pleasant surprise. If you take the time to find superior oils and use them in ways that enhance their natural characteristics, you will open up a whole new realm of cooking that is not only delicious, but also simple and healthy, too. The recipes in this section demonstrate ways in which an oil can be a primary element in a dish. Most of these recipes feature olive oil for the simple reason that, when an oil is the dominant flavor, olive oil is almost always the best choice. Certain oils stand out as exceptions—toasted sesame, walnut, and hazelnut oils, especially. Some make an appearance here, though they are more fully represented in the section, The Union of Opposites (pages 165–239), where they are joined with vinegars in a variety combinations.

LITTLE RECIPES

Popcorn Pop corn in pure olive oil and, when it is done, toss it with extra virgin olive oil, freshly grated Romano or Parmesan cheese, and salt and pepper.

Southwest Popcorn For an unusual taste and appearance, pop blue corn in refined corn oil and, when it is done, toss it with unrefined corn oil, chili powder, salt, and some cayenne pepper.

Marinated Mozzarella Cover thin strips of fresh mozzarella cheese with extra virgin olive oil. It will keep refrigerated for several days and is wonderful on an *antipasti* platter or served with fresh sliced tomatoes (in season, please!). Remove the cheese from the refrigerator 30 minutes before serving. Also delicious is feta cheese or small rounds of *chèvre* prepared and served in the same way. Garlic lovers should add several minced garlic cloves to any of the versions.

Bread & Oil Instead of butter, serve a bowl of specialty extra virgin olive oil with hot bread. Have salt and pepper available, or sprinkle some directly onto the bowl of olive oil. Guests dip their bread directly into the bowl of oil.

Summer Sandwich To add a bright spark of heat to a sandwich of summer tomatoes, red onion, and garlic mayonnaise, drizzle a tablespoon of mustard oil over the sandwich before adding the second slice of bread.

Pizza When making pizza at home, spread a liberal amount of olive oil over the surface of your shaped dough and top with your favorite ingredients: fresh sliced tomatoes in season, fresh mozzarella cheese, garlic, and basil; thin slices of sautéed eggplant, sliced black or *Kalamata* olives, and roasted peppers; puréed, sun-dried tomatoes (in oil), sautéed scallions, and goat feta or *chèvre*; sautéed onions, rosemary, and Gorgonzola cheese; sautéed wild mushrooms, shallots, and Gruyère cheese. Bake as usual.

Spaghetti with Olive Oil, Nutmeg, & Black Pepper Cook and drain ½ pound thin spaghetti. After draining, immediately toss with enough extra virgin olive oil to coat it liberally. Add 2 teaspoons fresh ground black pepper, 1 teaspoon ground nutmeg, and ½ teaspoon salt. Served with a simple green salad, this is superb eating in record time.

Baked Potatoes Pour 2 tablespoons or more of your favorite olive oil onto a baked potato. Add some black pepper and salt and you are ready to eat.

Vanilla Oil Split open a vanilla bean, place it in a bottle (a wine bottle works perfectly) and cover it with a good oil—walnut, hazelnut, or a very mild olive oil—and let it stand for 1 week. Use it in vinaigrettes that call for vanilla (see page 221), drizzle it on fruit salad, or use it to make vanilla mayonnaise. As you use the original oil, top up the bottle with fresh oil and the vanilla bean will continue to flavor it.

White Truffle Oil Try a few drops of this intensely flavored olive oil on grilled steak or *carpaccio* of beef, tuna, or salmon.

BREADS

 *Croutons*

Makes 3 cups

This is a simple, foolproof method for making great croutons with a minimum of fuss. The quantities can easily be adjusted, and aromatics and spices can be added to accommodate specific recipes.

½ to ¾ cup extra virgin olive oil

3 cups cubes of fresh sourdough bread (see Note below)

Note: Day-old bread works perfectly well in this recipe.

Place the olive oil in a large jar that has a lid. Add the cubes of bread, close the container, and shake it until the bread has absorbed all the oil and the cubes are evenly coated. Place the bread cubes on a baking sheet and bake in a 250°F. oven until the croutons are golden and dry. Cool, use immediately, or store in an air-tight container.

VARIATIONS
PEPPER CROUTONS After the croutons have absorbed the oil, add 1 to 2 teaspoons finely crushed black pepper and shake until it has been evenly distributed.

GARLIC CROUTONS Press 3 or 4 cloves of garlic into the oil and shake well before adding the bread cubes.

CHEESE CROUTONS After shaking the croutons with the oil, add ½ cup freshly grated Parmesan cheese to the jar and shake again to distribute the cheese evenly.

 # Bruschetta

Serves 4

A traditional Italian recipe, bruschetta is a terrific way to highlight the taste of a particularly special hearty olive oil as there are few other ingredients to compete with its taste. Ideally, bruschetta should be grilled over a wood fire, but that is not essential. Stove-top grills are fine, a ridged cast-iron skillet will work in a pinch, and you can even use a toaster oven. Get your guests involved in the process by having them rub the garlic onto the bread themselves. Serve bruschetta with a light and fruity red wine.

½ loaf sourdough Italian bread or any good, crusty bread
4 large cloves garlic, peeled and halved

½ to ¾ cup extra virgin olive oil
Coarse-grained salt
Black pepper, freshly ground

Cut the bread, on the diagonal, into ¾-inch slices. Grill the bread until it is well browned on both sides. Remove the bread from the grill and rub each piece with the cut garlic. Place the bread on a serving platter, drizzle the slices with the olive oil, and sprinkle with a little coarse salt and black pepper. Serve immediately, passing more olive oil on the side if you like.

Pepper Bruschetta
with Fresh Mozzarella Cheese

Serves 8

Sonoma County, where I make my home, is blessed with exquisite agricultural products as well as chefs, bakers, and cheesemakers whose talents transform the raw products into wonderful foods. I combine two of those here—Three-Pepper Bread from Brother Juniper's Bakery and fresh mozzarella di capri from Redwood Hill Farm Goat Dairy—to create an embellished version of traditional bruschetta. If these products are not available to you, substitute your favorite country-style bread and any fresh mozzarella cheese. To add to the bite offered by the Pepper Bread, add a sprinkling of red pepper flakes.

1 unsliced, 1-pound baguette of Three-Pepper Bread or other country-style bread
6 to 8 cloves garlic, peeled and cut in half
About 4 ounces fresh mozzarella cheese or mozzarella di capri, thinly sliced

1 cup extra virgin olive oil
Salt and pepper
10 large opal basil leaves, cut in a chiffonade (optional)
1 or 2 sprigs opal basil for garnish (optional)

Cut the bread, on the diagonal, in ¾-inch slices. Grill the bread until it is well browned on 1 side. Remove the bread from the grill, rub the grilled side of each piece with the cut garlic, and top it with a slice of the cheese. Return the bread to the grill until the other side is toasted and the cheese has melted. Remove the bread to a large serving platter, drizzle the slices with the olive oil, and sprinkle them with a little coarse salt and black pepper. If you are using the basil, sprinkle it over the *bruschetta* and garnish the platter with the basil sprigs. Serve immediately, passing more olive oil on the side if you like.

Pizza
with Roasted Vegetables, Olive Oil, and Fresh Herbs

Makes two 10-inch pizzas; serves 4 to 6

DOUGH

¼ ounce dry yeast
  (1 package)
1½ cups warm water
4½ cups all-purpose flour

1 teaspoon salt
2 generous tablespoons
  extra virgin olive oil

TOPPING

3 Japanese or Chinese eggplants
2 small, mature green zucchini or 1 cup baby
  green zucchini
2 small, mature yellow
  zucchini or 1 cup baby
  yellow zucchini
1 cup red pearl onions or
  6 baby torpedo onions,
  skin and stem ends
  removed

16 shiitake mushrooms,
  about 2 inches in dia-
  meter, stems removed
6 cloves garlic
2 teaspoons seasalt
1 cup extra virgin olive oil
8 slices fresh mozzarella
  or 2 cups grated
  cheese: Gruyère,
  Fontina, or fresh Asiago
¼ cup chopped fresh
  herbs

To begin the dough, place the yeast and ¼ cup of the warm water in a mixing bowl and set it aside for 10 minutes. Stir in the remaining water and 1 cup flour. Add the salt and olive oil and stir. Add the remaining flour, cup by cup, mixing each completely before adding the next until you have just ½ cup left. Turn the dough out onto a floured surface and knead until it is smooth and velvety, about 7 minutes, working in as much of the remaining flour as the dough will take. Place the dough in a clean bowl well coated with olive oil. Cover with a damp towel, set in a warm place, and let it rise for 2 hours.

While the dough is rising, prepare the vegetables. Remove the stems ends from the eggplant and mature zucchini and cut them lengthwise into ¼-inch-thick slices. If you are using baby zucchini, simply rinse them and pat them dry. Place all of the eggplant, zucchini, onions, and mushrooms in a large bowl. In a mortar and pestle, pound together the garlic and salt until smooth. Combine it in a small bowl with the olive oil and drizzle about half of the mixture over the vegetables. Toss them and set the bowl aside.

Punch the dough down, let it rest for 5 minutes, and form it into two 10-inch pizza shells. While the dough is resting, grill the vegetables on a stove-top grill for about 2 or 3 minutes on each side. If you do not have a grill, roast them in a hot oven for 15 minutes. After you have formed the pizza shells, spread the surface of each with enough of the remaining garlic and olive oil to cover. Place the cheese over the surface and top with an attractive arrangement of the grilled or roasted vegetables. Top with the fresh herbs.

Bake the pizzas at 450°F. for 15 minutes, or until the crust is golden. Use a pizza stone if you have one; otherwise, use a baking sheet. Remove from the oven, cut each pizza into 8 slices, and serve with a cruet of olive oil on the side.

Avocado Soup
with Radishes & Cilantro Cream

Serves 4 to 6

Avocados have a mildly nutty flavor that is enhanced by the use of walnut oil in this recipe. Avocado oil itself also has a nutty, rather than a fruity flavor and is a good choice for this recipe. You can make the soup and the cilantro cream a day in advance, but it is best to prepare the radishes just an hour or two before serving, so that they remain pleasantly crisp. This refreshing soup is ideal on a hot summer night.

2 tablespoons avocado oil and 1 tablespoon walnut oil or 3 tablespoons fruity olive oil

1 medium yellow onion, chopped

4 cloves garlic, peeled and minced

1 piece of ginger, 1½ inches long, peeled and minced

3 serrano or jalapeño chili peppers, stemmed, seeded, and minced

4 cups chicken stock

3 ripe avocados, preferably the Haas variety

2 limes

½ cup sour cream

2 tablespoons half-and-half

¼ cup cilantro leaves, very finely minced

1 teaspoon ground coriander

Salt

10 to 12 radishes, 1 standard bunch

Black pepper

Heat the avocado oil or two tablespoons of the olive oil in a saucepan and add the chopped onion. Sauté for 5 minutes and add the garlic, ginger, and 2 of the peppers. Sauté for another 5 minutes. Add the stock, simmer for 10 minutes, and remove from heat.

While the stock and vegetables are simmering, cut the avocados in half, and seed and peel them. Chop the avocados, toss them with the juice of 1 lime, and place about half the avocado in a blender container. Add hot stock and vegetables until container is about ¾ full and process until the mixture is smooth and liquid. Repeat with remaining avocado and stock. Chill the soup thoroughly, preferably for several hours.

To make the cilantro cream, stir the sour cream and half-and-half together, add the chopped cilantro, the remaining chili pepper, the ground coriander, and salt to taste. Chill until you are ready to use it.

Cut the radishes in small *julienne* and toss with the walnut oil or the remaining olive oil, the juice of ½ lime, and salt to taste. Chill until you are ready to use them.

Taste the chilled soup and add salt and more lime juice to taste. Ladle it into chilled soup bowls. Top each serving with a tablespoon of cilantro cream and a tablespoon of *julienned* radishes.

VARIATION
This soup is also delicious when served hot and is an ideal opening to a hearty Mexican meal.

Tuscan White Bean Soup

Serves 4

There are more complex versions of this hearty, traditional soup, some that include ham hocks, one in which the soup is poured over thick slices of olive oil–drenched bread. I developed this simplified version to show off a fabulous olive oil I carried home from the hill country east of Siena, Italy. The deep green oil sparkles in little pools on the white canvas of the soup, offering a delicate feast for the eye as well as the palate.

1 pound cannellini beans or Great Northerns or small whites	1 ½ cups freshly grated imported Parmesan cheese (see Note below)
1 onion, white or yellow, peeled and chopped	1 tablespoon fresh, cracked black pepper
8 large cloves garlic, peeled	1 teaspoon salt
	¼ cup extra virgin olive oil

Note: *Pecorino* or Romano cheese also give excellent results in this soup.

Rinse the beans under cool water. Place them in a heavy pot and add water to cover by an inch. Bring the beans to a boil, remove them from the heat, and let them sit for 1 hour. Drain the beans and rinse them well. Return them to the pot and cover with water. Simmer the beans for 20 minutes. Drain, rinse them again, return them to the pot, and cover them with fresh water. Add the whole cloves of garlic and the chopped onion and simmer the mixture over low heat until the beans are very tender, adding more water as necessary to keep them from sticking to the pot.

Purée the mixture, adding more water to provide a good consistency for soup. Add cheese, pepper, and salt. Stir well to blend, and warm over low heat until the cheese is melted and incorporated into the soup. Taste the mixture and correct the seasoning. Serve immediately, drizzling a tablespoon or two of extra virgin olive oil over each portion.

This soup will keep well, properly refrigerated, for several days.

Garlic Soup
with Fresh Herbs & Garlic Croutons

Serves 4 to 6

Make this delicately creamy soup only when fresh herbs and high-quality garlic are available. That leaves the late winter months, when the summer crop of garlic has lost its vibrancy and before the first spring garlic is available, to be spent longing for the rich broth, but then there is nothing like expectation to whet the appetite.

1 ½ quarts hearty chicken
  stock
2 cups garlic cloves, peeled
1 ¼ cups fresh herbs,
  loosely packed (a mix-
  ture of Italian parsley,
  thyme, oregano, chives,
  rosemary, marjoram,
  sage, and savory)

½ cup heavy cream
1 ½ cups freshly grated
  Asiago cheese
Salt and freshly ground
  black pepper
Garlic croutons (page 87)
Aïoli (page 234)

Place the chicken stock, garlic, and 1 cup of the fresh herbs in a heavy pot and bring the mixture to a boil. Reduce the heat and simmer until the garlic is soft, about 20 minutes. Purée the mixture and strain it through a sieve. Return the strained soup to the pan, add the cream, half of the cheese, and salt and pepper to taste. Heat the soup, but do not let it come to a boil.

To serve, ladle the soup into preheated bowls. Add several croutons to each serving, along with a sprinkling of the remaining cheese and herbs. Top each serving with a spoonful of *aïoli* and serve immediately.

Roasted Carrot & Coconut Soup
Serves 4 to 6

The slow roasting of the carrots and shallots, lubricated liberally with olive oil, draws out their natural sweetness beautifully. You can find coconut cream and coconut milk in Asian markets, gourmet shops, and in bar condiment sections of liquor stores and supermarkets, where they are available for piña coladas.

1 pound organic carrots, trimmed and cleaned well

2 or 3 shallots, peeled

¼ cup olive oil

1 piece of fresh ginger, ½ an inch long, peeled and minced

2 teaspoons ground cumin

3 cups chicken stock or vegetable stock

1 cup coconut milk

¼ cup coconut cream

Juice of 1 lime

1 ½ cups plain yogurt

1 teaspoon toasted cumin seed

Fresh cilantro

Coat the carrots and peeled shallots liberally with the olive oil and place them in a roasting pan in a 350°F. oven. Roast until tender, about 45 minutes, turning them once or twice to prevent their burning. Remove the vegetables from the oven, cool them, and chop them coarsely. Heat the remaining olive oil in a heavy saucepan and sauté the roasted vegetables and minced ginger for 3 or 4 minutes. Add the ground cumin and chicken stock and simmer over low heat for 20 minutes. Purée the mixture and strain it through a fine sieve. Return it to the saucepan, stir in the coconut milk, coconut cream, lime juice, and ¾ cup of the yogurt. Taste and add more yogurt if desired. Heat the soup, but do not boil it after the addition of the coconut milk. Ladle the soup into hot soup bowls and garnish each serving with a spoonful of yogurt, toasted cumin seeds, and cilantro leaves.

Garden Minestrone

You should vary the ingredients of this soup depending on the season. You can make it in the spring, when the first peas ripen. Try it again when the zucchini are still tiny, about as big as your little finger, and the first Blue Lake green beans beckon. The marvelous thing about this soup, really, is that it is good any time you make it, and rich and nourishing without being heavy.

1 cup olive oil
1 yellow onion, peeled and diced
3 carrots, trimmed and diced
2 leeks, trimmed with just 2 inches of green remaining and thinly sliced
1 stalk celery, diced
1 ½ pounds fresh Roma tomatoes, peeled and sliced or 1 can, 28 ounces, whole tomatoes, sliced
1 pound small new red potatoes cut into medium dice
2 quarts beef stock

¼ pound pancetta or bacon
1 head garlic, cloves separated, peeled, and minced
3 tablespoons Italian parsley, finely chopped
1 tablespoon fresh oregano
1 pound baby zucchini or 4 small to medium zucchini
2 cups cooked cannellini beans
One of the following combinations: 1 cup fresh spring peas and ¼ pound haricot verts (very young Blue Lake

green beans) or 2 cups (lightly packed) sliced Swiss chard and 6 to 8 ounces small dried pasta, such as orzo, rosemarina, small shells, or tripolini

Salt and pepper
4 ounces freshly grated Asiago cheese

Heat the olive oil in a large, heavy soup pot. Add the onion, carrots, leeks, and celery and sauté until the vegetables are very soft. Add the tomatoes, potatoes, and the beef stock and simmer until the potatoes are almost tender. Dice the *pancetta* or bacon and sauté it in a little olive oil until it begins to brown. Add the minced garlic, sauté for another 2 minutes, add the parsley and oregano, remove from the heat, and add to the soup mixture, along with the zucchini, *cannellini*, and peas and beans or chard and pasta. Simmer until the pasta is tender, about 7 to 10 minutes, depending on the size of the pasta. Remove the soup from the heat and let it rest until ready to serve. Correct the seasoning with salt and pepper, heat, and serve in hot soup bowls. Garnish with Asiago cheese.

VARIATION
During basil season, add a little fresh chopped basil to the soup and top each serving with a spoonful of *pesto* (page 108) instead of the cheese.

Perfect French Fries

Serves 3 to 4

It does not hurt to know how to make great French fries, unless, of course, you abuse the knowledge by making them as often as you would like. The secret to making perfect French fries is the double frying, which results in the ideal texture, color, and temperature. They are delicious, one of those guilty pleasures that should be indulged occasionally. They are excellent sprinkled with just a little malt or cider vinegar, heavenly dipped into a powerful aïoli, and, of course, there is nothing quite like French fries and ketchup. Try them with the Peach Ketchup on page 141.

1 pound mature russet (baking) potatoes
Refined vegetable oil: safflower, corn, peanut, canola, or, for a little more flavor, olive (the quantity of oil you will need will depend on the size of your container for frying)

Wash the potatoes well, but do not peel them. Cut the potatoes into lengths measuring approximately ⅜ inch square and between 3 and 4 inches long. Soak them in cold water for at least 1 hour. Remove them from their water bath and drain them on a tea towel, not paper towels, small fragments of which might cling to the potatoes. Pour between 3 and 4 inches of oil into a heavy cooking pot and raise the temperature of the oil slowly to about 340°F. Carefully plunge about 1 cup—a good-sized handful—of the cut potatoes into the oil and jiggle the pot or stir the potatoes slightly with a heavy spoon to ensure that they do not stick to one another. Let the potatoes fry for about 4 minutes and then remove them to drain on several layers of paper toweling or on a brown grocery bag. A deep fryer with a basket is helpful in the process, but not essential. Repeat the process until all of the potatoes have been fried once. Let the fried potatoes rest and cool.

You may stop the recipe at this point. When you are ready to finish cooking, return the oil to between 350° and 360°F. Fry the potatoes in batches a second time, leaving them in the hot oil until they are beautifully golden, about 3 to 4 minutes. Remove the potatoes from the pot, drain them, and place them in a basket or on a platter. Season with a little salt and serve immediately with your favorite French fry condiment.

Algerian Carrots

Serves 4; the variation serves 8 to 10

I learned to make these delicious carrots at the right hand of Hubert Saulnier, owner and chef of the tiny bistro, A Chez Nous, now a part of culinary history here in Sonoma County. Carrots in a slightly sweet dressing and zucchini in a very garlicky dressing were served together as a complimentary appetizer with all meals, a dish so loved by the clientele that there were many who came to dine just on these very good vegetables. Even my daughter Gina, with her temperamental palate, loved them.

With a loaf of French bread and a glass of wine, they make a wonderful light meal, served warm or chilled. The carrots by themselves make a perfect vegetable accompaniment to meats, poultry, rice, and pasta dishes.

1 pound carrots, peeled	1 lemon
¼ cup extra virgin olive oil	1 tablespoon minced
2 teaspoons ground cumin	Italian parsley
1 teaspoon brown sugar	Salt
3 cloves garlic, minced	

Cut the carrots at an angle to make slices about ⅛-inch thick. Steam the carrots until they are just tender, about 10 minutes; do not overcook them. Place the olive oil, cumin, and brown sugar in a bowl and mix together. Remove the carrots from the heat and let them cool slightly. Place the carrots and the garlic in the bowl with the olive oil mixture and toss until the carrots are well coated. Squeeze the juice of half of the lemon over the carrots; add the parsley and a pinch of salt. Taste the mixture and add the remaining lemon juice and more salt if desired.

VARIATION

Prepare an equal quantity of zucchini, cooking the vegetable until it is very tender. Drain the cooked zucchini in a strainer or colander for 15 minutes. In a separate bowl (the carrots and zucchini are not mixed at all), combine ¼ cup olive oil, 4 to 5 teaspoons cumin, and 6 to 8 cloves garlic, minced. Omit the brown sugar and parsley. Add more lemon juice and salt to taste. Serve the carrots and zucchini alongside each other. The combination is sensational.

Baked Eggplant

When eggplant is cooked long enough and slowly enough, with plenty of good olive oil, it is a wonderful food, a creamy accompaniment to poultry, meats, and many grains. Initially, eggplant will absorb an enormous quantity of oil, which you should just let it do. As it cooks, it will eventually give up a lot of the oil it has absorbed, which makes draining the eggplant after cooking essential.

1 large eggplant or 4 Chinese, Japanese, or Italian eggplants	Fresh mozzarella or mozzarella di capra
¾ cup olive oil	Salt and black pepper

Cut the eggplant lengthwise, from stem tip to end, in ⅜-inch slices. If you are using a whole large eggplant, place the slices in a colander, sprinkle them with 1 teaspoon salt, and let the eggplant sit for 30 minutes so that the excess moisture leaches out.

Pour about ⅓ of a cup of olive oil on a small baking sheet. Set the slices of eggplant on top and drizzle them with the rest of the olive oil, coating each slice well. Place in a 325°F. oven and bake until soft and creamy, about 20 to 30 minutes, depending on the type of eggplant used. Remove them from the oven and drain on absorbent paper. Serve warm, seasoned with salt and pepper, and topped with a slice of mozzarella.

VARIATION

This version works best with large eggplant. Sauté ¾ pound ground lamb with 6 cloves minced garlic, 1 teaspoon crushed oregano, the juice of half a lemon, salt, and pepper. Slice 1 large or 2 small ripe tomatoes into rounds. Top each slice of cooked eggplant with a slice of tomato, a healthy helping of lamb, and 2 slices of mozzarella. Place the assembled eggplant slices in a hot oven until the cheese has melted.

CONDIMENTS & SAUCES

Flavored Olive Oil

In 1991, flavored oils, or oil infusions as they also are called, became the new darlings of the culinary world. Chefs splatter brightly colored oils on plates like Jackson Pollock once splattered paint on canvas. Sometimes the oils offer a bright flash of flavor to a dish; more often the contribution is visual, especially if an inferior oil is used, as it often is. If a good-tasting oil is used, it can add a nice touch to soups, stews, beans, and grilled meats and seafood. Drizzle on a tablespoon or so just before serving. Basil is probably the most commonly used flavoring, with sun-dried tomatoes a close second. I find cilantro, sage, and oregano more interesting, and rosemary is my favorite. I use it sparingly atop gravlax (salt-cured salmon) with a little sour cream added.

1 cup fresh herbs (see
   Note next page)

2 cups extra virgin olive
   oil
Salt and pepper

Place the herbs in a blender container and add half of the oil. Process until the herbs have been completely pulverized. Pour the herb and oil blend into a glass container, add the remaining oil, and refrigerate for 1 day. Strain the mixture through a fine sieve lined with cheesecloth. Season the strained oil with just enough salt and pepper to bring up the flavor of the herb. Store in the refrigerator until ready to use.

Note: Flavored oils are best made with a single herb, not a combination. To set their color, the herbs should be blanched in boiling water for about 45 seconds and then shocked in an ice water bath, remaining there until fully cooled. Drain the herbs and dry them well before placing them in the blender. Sundried tomatoes (dry, not marinated) should be dropped in boiling water, simmered for two minutes, and drained before using.

Southern Bath
A Sauce for Grilled Seafood, Vegetables, & Bread
Makes approximately 2 cups

This sauce evolved from the Italian bagna cauda, *which literally means "hot bath" and is the name given to the garlicky butter and olive oil sauce into which one dips sliced vegetables and chunks of bread. I tried some of the sauce on grilled oysters one day and was pleased by the combination. The addition of Tabasco sauce was a simple next step, since the tart-hot sauce goes so well with raw oysters. Although at first glance three tablespoons may seem an excessive amount of Tabasco, it is not particularly fiery. This sauce is excellent on all types of grilled seafood, grilled vegetables, and bread and will keep, refrigerated, for several weeks.*

½ pound butter

1 head garlic, cloves separated, peeled, and minced

1 cup extra virgin olive oil

1 or 2 anchovy fillets, packed in oil

3 tablespoons Tabasco sauce (more or less to taste)

Melt the butter in a heavy saucepan until it is foamy. Add the garlic and simmer for 2 minutes. Add the olive oil and anchovies and simmer for another 2 minutes. Stir in the Tabasco sauce, taste, and add more sauce as desired. Spoon a small amount over barbecued oysters.

Stinking Rose Petals
Preserved Garlic Cloves

Makes 1½ cups

Garlic simmered slowly in duck fat, especially the fat from a smoked duck, is heavenly. It is nearly as delicious when pork fat is used. But, whatever you use, it is difficult to ignore considerations about animal fat and cholesterol. Use olive oil and you can indulge with abandon, knowing that the garlic and the olive oil may work hand in hand to keep those arteries unobstructed little passageways. Try serving preserved garlic spooned over the top of sliced fresh tomatoes or alongside grilled meats or seafood. Once the garlic has been used, save the olive oil for marinades and vinaigrettes or to drizzle over bruschetta for an added depth of flavor.

1 cup large garlic cloves, peeled and left whole

Extra virgin olive oil to cover

Place the garlic cloves in a small, heavy saucepan and simmer them over very low heat until they are tender, about 30 minutes. Remove from the heat and cool the mixture until you can handle it easily. You may serve it immediately with hot bread or store it for future use. Place the cloves in a jar, cover them with the olive oil, and refrigerate. Remove the garlic from the refrigerator at least 30 minutes before you are ready to use it, and serve it either at room temperature or warmed over a low flame.

 Pesto

Makes approximately 2 cups

No discussion of olive oil recipes would be complete without pesto. The simple purée of fresh basil, olive oil, garlic, and cheese is one of the classic uses of olive oil. Not only is it virtually impossible to make pesto without olive oil, but also it is essential that you use a good olive oil, full of natural good flavors. If, when you are making pesto, your basil needs rinsing, be sure to dry it thoroughly before beginning. If you will be storing your pesto, cover the exposed surface area with olive oil to prevent discoloration.

4 cups packed, fresh basil
   leaves
8 to 12 cloves garlic,
   peeled
¾ cup extra virgin olive oil
5 tablespoons softened
   butter

¾ cup freshly grated imported Parmesan cheese
4 tablespoons freshly
   grated pecorino
   Romano cheese
½ cup pine nuts

Place the basil leaves in a food processor or blender container. Add the garlic and turn on the machine at medium speed. Slowly pour in ½ cup of the olive oil, stopping as necessary to scrape the basil from the sides of the container. When the basil is finely puréed, transfer the mixture to a mixing bowl or freezer containers.

To freeze the purée, place it in single-portion containers, the amount you would use in 1 recipe. Large ice cube trays work well. Freezer bags do not work as well because too much surface area is exposed. After packing your basil into containers, cover it with a thin float of olive oil. This will decrease any darkening due to oxidation. When you are ready to use the basil, remove a portion from the freezer and add the remaining ingredients, adjusting quantities as necessary.

To continue with the *pesto* recipe, beat the softened butter into the basil mixture. Add the cheeses and blend well. Adjust the consistency by adding part or all of the remaining olive oil. Stir in the whole pine nuts. If you will not be using the *pesto* immediately, or if you have some left over, place it in a glass jar and cover the surface with a thin layer of olive oil.

To serve the *pesto* over pasta or fish, thin it with a tablespoon or two of hot water. *Pesto* should not be cooked.

Tuna Tapenade

Makes approximately 2 cups

Maggie Klein deserves credit for this recipe, although I have altered it from its original form in The Feast of the Olive. *A paste of olives and anchovies,* tapenade *has its roots in Provence, although variations abound wherever olives are part of the culinary terrain. I serve this version most often with very simple bread or crackers, but it is also an excellent accompaniment to grilled torpedo onions and as a filling in lavosh sandwiches.*

4 or 5 anchovy fillets, packed in oil

1 can (6½ ounces) tuna, packed in spring water, drained

3 large cloves garlic, peeled

1 tablespoon minced Italian parsley

1 cup Kalamata olives, pitted

½ cup extra virgin olive oil

¼ cup finely chopped red onion

¼ cup capers

1 hard-boiled egg, finely grated

Sprigs of Italian parsley

Kalamata olives for garnish

Place the anchovies, tuna, garlic, parsley, and pitted olives in a food processor or blender. Blend the mixture until it is smooth and, with the motor still running, drizzle in the olive oil. The *tapenade* should be smooth, similar in consistency to mayonnaise.

To serve, place the *tapenade* in a bowl or crock. Place the onions, capers, and egg in small bowls and set them nearby. Garnish the *tapenade* with a sprinkling of each of the condiments, a sprig or two of parsley, and a few of the olives. Serve with bread, croutons, or crackers.

The *tapenade* keeps well refrigerated, though it should be removed 30 minutes before serving and stirred to reincorporate any oil that has settled out.

DESSERTS

Corn Biscotti

Makes approximately 5 dozen 2½-inch cookies

Corn plays a triple role in these light and crunchy cookies. Polenta provides the texture, unrefined corn oil offers a subtle note of good flavor, and whole kernels of corn add a pleasing visual element as well as a bright spark of taste. If unrefined corn oil proves difficult to find, you can make these cookies with a neutral flavored oil, regular corn oil, perhaps, or peanut oil.

3 cups all-purpose flour
1½ cups polenta (coarse
   ground corn meal)
¾ cup sugar
2½ teaspoons baking
   powder
½ teaspoon salt
3 eggs, beaten

⅓ cup unrefined corn oil
1½ teaspoons vanilla
   extract
1 cup fresh or frozen
   small corn kernels
1 egg white, mixed with 1
   tablespoon water

Combine the dry ingredients—the flour, polenta, sugar, baking powder, and salt—in a large mixing bowl. Mix together the eggs, corn oil, and vanilla extract. Add the egg mixture to the dry ingredients and beat either by hand or with an electric mixer until the dough is smooth. Stir in the fresh or frozen corn by hand.

Preheat oven to 400°F. and lightly butter and flour a baking sheet. Dust your work surface with a generous quantity of flour. With well-floured hands, remove a piece of dough about the size of a tennis ball. Using your palms, roll it into a rope about 2 inches in diameter and about 10 inches long. Use as much flour as necessary to keep the rope of dough from sticking to the work surface. The dough will be soft. Quickly, so that it does not stretch, place the rope on your prepared baking sheet. Repeat the process, leaving at least 2½ inches between rows, until the sheet is filled. Brush the ropes with the egg white mixture and bake for 20 minutes.

Remove the cookie ropes from the oven and cool them on racks for 5 minutes. Cut each rope diagonally into ¾-inch-thick slices. Arrange the sliced cookies on a clean, dry baking sheet, cut-side down, lower the oven temperature to 325°F. and return the cookies to the oven for another 7 to 10 minutes, until they are very dry. Allow the *biscotti* to cool on a drying rack and store them in a closed container.

Walnut
& Black Pepper Biscotti

Makes between 3½ and 4 dozen cookies

Biscotti, twice-baked cookies of Italian origin, are wonderfully simple to make, with a final result that is not only delicious but also very satisfying. This version, with its scent of walnuts and the mildest whisper of black pepper, is delicious with Gelato Modena *(page 162) and* Strawberries & Black Pepper *(page 119).*

3 tablespoons walnut oil
2 eggs
1 cup dark brown sugar, firmly packed
1 teaspoon fresh cracked black pepper

2 cups all-purpose flour
1 teaspoon baking soda
¼ teaspoon nutmeg
1 cup coarsely chopped walnuts, lightly toasted

Preheat your oven to 375°F. and butter and flour a baking sheet. Beat together the oil and the eggs, add the sugar and pepper, and beat until the ingredients are well combined. Set the mixture aside. Combine the flour, baking soda, and nutmeg. Slowly add the dry ingredients to the sugar mixture. Add the walnuts to the dough, which will be fairly stiff but sticky.

Flour your work surface, divide the dough in thirds, and form each piece into a rope about 12 inches long and 2½ inches in diameter. Place the ropes of dough on the baking sheet about 2½ or 3 inches apart. Using your fingertips, flatten the top of each rope slightly. Bake for 25 minutes.

Remove the loaves from the oven and allow them to cool on racks for about 5 minutes. Cut each warm loaf diagonally into slices ½ inch wide. Place the slices on a cookie sheet, cut-side down, and return them to the oven for about 20 minutes. Turn the *biscotti* after 10 minutes. Cool on racks and store in an air-tight jar.

VARIATION

To make hazelnut *biscotti*, use hazelnut oil, hazelnuts—toasted and peeled—and ½ teaspoon vanilla extract; omit the black pepper.

Olive Oil & Red Wine Biscotti

Makes about 60 cookies, measuring about 1 inch by 2½ inches

These cookies, with their rosy hue and subtle hint of wine, have become a favorite around my house. Stored in a jar or tin, they keep well and make excellent holiday gifts.

1 egg
1 cup pure olive oil
¾ cup sugar
1 teaspoon pure vanilla
   extract
2 cups whole wheat flour
3 cups all-purpose flour
2 teaspoons baking powder

½ teaspoon salt
1 cup red wine, such as
   Cabernet Sauvignon,
   Zinfandel, Pinot Noir,
   or Merlot
1 ½ cups walnuts, toasted
   and chopped (optional)

Beat the egg until it is creamy. Add the olive oil, beat it with the egg until the mixture becomes just slightly foamy, and then add the sugar and vanilla. Combine the ingredients well and set the mixture aside. In a separate bowl, combine the flours, baking powder, and salt. Add this mixture to the egg and oil mixture, a fourth at a time and alternately with ¼ portions of the wine. Mix until the final addition is well blended and the dough is stiff. If you are using the walnuts, work them in with your hands in a quick kneading motion.

Divide the dough into quarters and work each piece into a rope about 10 inches long and 1½ inches in diameter. Place the ropes of dough at least 2 inches apart on a greased baking sheet and flatten them just slightly with your fingers. Bake for 25 minutes at 375°F.

Remove the loaves from the oven and let them cool slightly on wire racks. Reduce the oven temperature to 325°F. Cut the warm loaves into diagonal slices about ⅜ inch thick and place them, cut-side up, on the baking sheet. Return to the oven for an additional 15 to 20 minutes, until the *biscotti* are very dry. Remove from the oven and let the *biscotti* dry on wire racks until they are completely cool. Store in a glass jar or tin.

Pumpkin Bar Cookies

Makes 48 cookies

Nick Sciabica & Sons is one of the four major producers of olive oil in California and, although large, it is without a doubt a family business. Gemma Sciabica's recipes feature the family's olive oil and the one she offers here illustrates the use of olive oil in a dessert that might traditionally call for butter.

4 eggs
1¾ cups sugar
⅓ cup virgin olive oil
1¾ cups cooked pumpkin, cooled
2¼ cups flour
2 teaspoons baking powder
1 teaspoon baking soda

¾ teaspoon salt
1 teaspoon ground cinnamon
¼ teaspoon each ground ginger, ground nutmeg, and ground cloves
½ cup raisins
½ cup chopped pecans

Preheat the oven to 350°F. and lightly butter a jelly-roll pan (measuring 15½ inches by 10½ inches by 1 inch). Beat together the eggs and sugar until light and foamy. Add the oil and pumpkin and mix well. Sift together the flour, baking powder, baking soda, salt, and spices. Quickly add the dry ingredients to the egg mixture, being sure not to overbeat the mixture. Fold in the raisins and nuts and pour the mixture into the prepared pan. Bake between 25 and 30 minutes. Remove from the oven and cool the cake before slicing it into 2-inches-by-1½-inch bars.

COOKING WITH VINEGAR

COOKING WITH VINEGAR IS ENTIRELY DIF-
ferent from cooking with oil. First of all, we have a very
strong reaction to simple acetic acid, and it is rarely pleasant
when used in substantial quantities, unmitigated by other
ingredients. We must learn to choose a vinegar wisely and
to use it judiciously, so that it enhances a particular dish and
contributes its uniquely tart flavor without dominating the
other ingredients. The Little Recipes that begin the section
show ways in which vinegar can stand on its own, making a
contribution in flavor so simple that it is often overlooked.
It functions in a similar, though somewhat more complex,
way in other key recipes in this section. *Mignonette* sauce is
the perfect example. You may serve oysters rarely but when
you do, a well-seasoned vinegar sauce will make those oysters a dazzling contribution to any special occasion.

Vinegar also plays a special role in the three recipes
for seafood cooked in parchment, adding an aromatic presence by flavoring the fish as it steams and creating a more
delicate taste than that we usually associate with vinegar. If
you hesitate to cook with parchment, these simple, flavorful
recipes may change your reluctance into enthusiasm.

The other recipes in this section demonstrate the vital-
ity of vinegar in our cuisine. It is essential in a variety of
condiments from ketchup to chutney. Its tartness, combined
with the flavors of its substrate, can draw out the natural
flavors of the other ingredients. In the Fall Fruit Gazpacho,

for instance, the sweetness of the rice vinegar plays up the sweetness of the fruit.

LITTLE RECIPES

Vinegar Spritzer Fill a 12-ounce glass with ice cubes and add sparkling water nearly to the top. Add 3 or 4 tablespoons of a low-acid (4.5 percent) fruit vinegar and 1 or 2 teaspoons balsamic vinegar. My favorite is raspberry vinegar, but blueberry, peach, and many others are delicious. The balsamic vinegar can be omitted entirely or even used by itself.

Vinegar as a Condiment Lightly sautéed vegetables are delicious with a splash of your favorite vinegar; so, too, a hearty soup is perked up by a sprinkling. Keep a cruet on the table where it is handy at all times.

John's Cold & Flu Tonic My editor, John Harris, claims that this really works; let me add that it also tastes great. To a cup of hot chicken broth, add 1 tablespoon white wine or champagne vinegar, 1 clove crushed garlic, and a few drops of Tabasco sauce. No sweat!

Anchovies in Vinegar Place 2 ounces of anchovy fillets (packed in oil) in a glass or porcelain bowl. Pour ¾ cup red wine vinegar over the anchovies and refrigerate until you are ready to use them. The anchovies, served with hot crusty bread and a glass of hearty red wine, make an ideal afternoon snack or prelude to a simple rustic dinner. The vinegar cuts through the salty intensity that some find objectionable in anchovies.

Garlic Conserve Coarsely chop 1 pound of peeled garlic cloves (about 8 heads) and place it in a nonreactive saucepan. Combine 1 cup balsamic vinegar, ½ cup white wine, and 1 cup sugar and pour the mixture over the garlic. Bring to a boil, reduce the heat, and simmer slowly until the garlic is soft and the mixture thick, about 30 minutes. Serve at room temperature with grilled meats, especially lamb. This recipe yields about 2 cups of conserve, which will keep, refrigerated, for 10 days.

Fresh Fruit with Vinegar Sprinkle sliced fresh fruit with a bit of vinegar and some black pepper. Fruit vinegars, sherry vinegars, rice vinegar, and balsamic vinegar are the best choices and go beautifully with nectarines, peaches, berries, and orange melons.

Strawberries & Black Pepper Toss 1 pint of sliced strawberries with 1 or 2 teaspoons of granulated sugar. Sprinkle with 2 tablespoons balsamic vinegar and several turns of black pepper. Chill and serve.

Fall Fruit Gazpacho

Serves 4

I love this soup on those scorching fall days when it is nearly too hot to eat. Served ice cold, it is refreshing, cooling, and elegantly evocative of childhood afternoons spent eating as much watermelon as my mother would let me have. For a particularly dramatic presentation, serve in scooped-out cantaloupe shells (leave about ¼ inch of the flesh), halved with a crown cut (see Note on next page).

3 cups yellow watermelon, seeded and cubed (use red watermelon if yellow is not available)

1 cup chopped orange melon, Crane, cantaloupe, or orange Honeydew

1 cup medium-dry white wine (Sauvignon Blanc is ideal) or champagne

1 serrano chili pepper, stem removed (optional)

4 cups ¼-inch cubes melon, any combination of cantaloupe, Honeydew, orange Honeydew, Crenshaw, Casaba, Crane, or red watermelon

Juice of half a lemon

2 tablespoons unseasoned rice vinegar or pineapple vinegar

4 or 5 peppermint leaves, cut into a very thin julienne

1 tablespoon minced cilantro leaves

¼ cup plain yogurt or crème fraîche

Small sprigs of mint and cilantro for garnish

¼ cup pomegranate seeds, if available

Place the yellow watermelon and the 1 cup of chopped orange melon in a blender or food processor, along with the wine. Add the *serrano* pepper if you want your *gazpacho* to have a spark of heat. Pulse the machine until the melon has been liquefied. Pour the mixture into a stainless steel or porcelain mixing bowl. Add the 4 cups cubed melon, lemon juice, rice vinegar, peppermint, and cilantro and stir lightly to blend. Chill for at least 2 hours before serving.

To serve, place the fruit *gazpacho* in chilled serving bowls. Garnish each serving with a teaspoon of yogurt or *crème fraîche*, a few leaves of mint and cilantro, and a scattering of pomegranate seeds. This soup will keep well for 2 to 3 days if properly refrigerated.

Note: To make a crown cut, which is a zigzag cut also known as lions' teeth or wolves' teeth, insert a knife at an angle near the "equator" of the melon through to the center of the melon. Repeat the process around the melon's circumference, alternating the slant of the knife with each insertion, until the melon has been cut in half. Pull the two sections apart and you should have two decorative halves with nicely spiked edges.

Red Raspberry Soup
with Smoked Chicken & Basil

Serves 4 to 6

Thick and creamy, yet light at the same time, this is a deceptively rich soup that is very low in fat. If you like the primary ingredients—raspberries, chicken, and basil—you will love this particular way of combining them.

1 ½ pints red raspberries
1 ½ cups chicken stock
2 tablespoons low-acid (4.5 percent) red raspberry vinegar
1 cup buttermilk
6 or 7 fresh basil leaves, cut in a thin julienne
1 to 3 tablespoons granulated sugar

2 cups smoked chicken meat, cut in a thin julienne
Freshly ground black pepper
Pinch salt
½ cup plain yogurt
Fresh basil leaves for garnish

Set aside ½ pint of berries. Place the remaining raspberries in a blender or food processor, along with the chicken stock and raspberry vinegar. Process until the mixture is smooth, strain through a fine sieve or cheesecloth, and place in a medium-sized bowl. Stir in the buttermilk and the basil. Add 1 tablespoon of sugar and taste the soup. Continue to add sugar in very small quantities, tasting between additions, until the soup has the right degree of sweetness, just enough to accent the berry flavor but not so sweet as to taste like a dessert soup. The amount will vary depending on the sweetness of the berries.

Add the chicken meat, reserved raspberries, several turns of black pepper, and a pinch of salt, and chill the soup for at least 1 hour before serving. To serve, ladle into chilled bowls and garnish with a generous spoonful of yogurt and a basil leaf. This soup is best served on the day it is made.

Kermit's Vinegar Eggs

Serves 1

Kermit Lynch, who is a wine merchant in Berkeley, California, and the author of Adventures on the Wine Route, *offered this recipe in one of his monthly newsletters. I love everything about it, the spirit in which it is written, the ingredients, and the underlying lust for good living it reveals, not to mention its taste. "This is not breakfast!" Kermit stresses.*

1 bottle good Beaujolais	**Salt and pepper**
2 eggs	**2 tablespoons red wine**
Butter	**vinegar**
	Bread

First you pour yourself a glass of cool Beaujolais. Then you fry fresh eggs slowly in butter, covered, until the whites are firm but the yolks remain runny. Add salt and pepper and then slide the eggs out onto a warm platter. Deglaze the pan with the vinegar and reduce it by half. Thicken the sauce with a slice of butter and pour it over your eggs. You will want bread or toast for sopping up the sauce. You will also want another glass of Beaujolais.

COOKING IN PARCHMENT

Cooking in parchment—also known as cooking en papillote—is simple and produces beautiful results, so do not be intimidated by the thought if you have never done it before.

Cooking parchment is available in better cookware stores and markets in sizes suitable for the home cook. It is also available in restaurant supply stores, generally in large sheets, 16 inches by 25 inches, that can easily be cut to size. Aluminum foil may be substituted, though the presentation is not nearly as dramatic and elegant as it is when the parchment is used.

Parchment cooking works best with foods that cook quickly. It is ideal for seafood, allowing it to steam in its own natural juices. A variety of additions can be made, though certain vegetables and pastas must be partially cooked first.

It is easy to form a parchment package:

1. Begin with a 12-inch-by-16-inch sheet of parchment and place it flat on your working surface. Smaller sheets of parchment can be used for appetizer portions.
2. Place the foods to be wrapped in the center of one half of the parchment, that is, in the middle of an area measuring 12 inches by 8 inches.
3. After you have filled the package, brush the outside rim of the parchment with oil or melted butter and fold it in half by bringing the 12-inch side farthest from you over to meet the 12-inch side closest to you.
4. Press around the edges so that the oil or butter will bond the parchment together.
5. To seal the parchment, begin folding in the upper left

corner. Make a deep, angular crease in the parchment by folding it toward the center. Repeat at intervals of 1½ or 2 inches until you have formed a semicircular package with the parchment.

6. Place the parchment packages on a baking sheet and refrigerate them until you are ready to bake them.

Oysters & Mushrooms in Parchment

Serves 4

The flavors of bacon, ginger, and rice vinegar join together to create a sensational, aromatic dish that is perfect with the oysters, which remain tender and plump during the quick cooking. To allow an evocative cloud of steam to entice your guests, make a tiny tear in each package as you serve it.

3 tablespoons unsalted butter
2 shallots, minced
½ pound shiitake mushrooms (or a combination of shiitakes and golden chanterelles)
1-inch piece fresh ginger, peeled and minced
Salt and pepper
4 slices bacon or pancetta

2 tablespoons finely chopped Italian parsley
16 oysters, shucked
4 teaspoons rice vinegar
2 limes, cut in wedges
4 sprigs Italian parsley
4 sprigs cilantro
4 sheets of cooking parchment, each measuring 12 inches by 16 inches

Melt the butter in a heavy skillet and sauté the shallots until they are soft and transparent. Clean the mushrooms, remove the stems of the *shiitakes*, and reserve them for soup or sauce. Slice the *shiitakes*, and if you are using them, break the *chanterelles* into medium-sized pieces (whole mushrooms or pieces up to 1½ inches across are fine). Add the mushrooms and ginger to the shallots, season with salt and pepper, add a splash of rice vinegar, cover, and let the mushrooms simmer gently until they are just limp. Uncover and remove from the heat to cool. Cook the bacon until it is just crisp, drain it on paper towels, crumble it, and set it aside.

Place the parchment on your working surface and divide the mushroom mixture evenly among the 4 sheets. Arrange 4 shucked oysters on top of each mound of mushrooms. Top with a sprinkling of the crushed bacon and chopped parsley, a hearty squeeze of lime juice, and about 1 teaspoon rice vinegar. Drape a small sprig of parsley and a small sprig of cilantro over the oysters and seal the packages (see page 124). Bake in a 400°F. oven for 5 or 6 minutes. Remove and serve immediately, garnished with parsley, cilantro, and a wedge of lime.

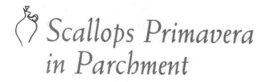

Scallops Primavera in Parchment

Serves 4

The following recipe is terrific for dinner parties. It can be prepared earlier in the day and refrigerated and takes just minutes to cook. It tastes really good, too, so your guests will be happy.

4 sheets cooking parchment, each measuring 12 inches by 16 inches
3 cups julienned vegetables, such as red pepper, yellow pepper, green beans, carrots, red onion
Salt
1-inch piece fresh ginger, peeled and minced
1 pound bay scallops
4 tablespoons compound butter (recipe follows)
4 sprigs Italian parsley
4 tablespoons rice vinegar
4 tablespoons white wine, Sauvignon Blanc or Chardonnay
Black pepper, freshly ground
2 lemons, cut in wedges
Sprigs of lavender and Italian parsley

Place the parchment flat on your work surface. On each sheet make a bed of the julienned vegetables and sprinkle them with salt and the chopped ginger. Place 4 scallops in the center and top them with a generous teaspoon of the compound butter. Place a parsley sprig over the top. Drizzle about 1 tablespoon each of the rice vinegar and white wine over the top, add a little more salt and a turn or two of black pepper, and seal the packages (see page 124). Refrigerate until just before cooking.

To cook, place the packages in a 375°F. oven until the parchment puffs up and browns slightly, about 7 minutes. Serve immediately, accompanied by wedges of lemon and garnish with the lavender and parsley.

VARIATION

For a heartier main course, cook ¼ pound dried angel hair pasta until two-thirds done and toss it with a little olive oil. To make the parchment packages, begin with a small bed of the pasta and then proceed with the vegetables and so on.

Compound Butter

¼ pound sweet butter, at room temperature

½ teaspoon grated orange zest

1 teaspoon Herbs de Provence (see Note below)

¼ teaspoon dried lavender flowers

1 clove garlic, finely minced

1 small shallot, finely minced

½ teaspoon sugar

Pinch salt

Pinch white pepper

Combine all the ingredients by hand or in a food processor until they are well blended. Taste, correct seasoning, and refrigerate until you are ready to use it.

Note: *Herbs de Provence* is a blend of dried savory herbs and usually includes thyme, oregano, summer savory, marjoram, and sometimes anise and lavender.

Blueberry Orange Roughy in Parchment

Serves 4

Orange roughy is a delicate, mild-flavored fish that is the ideal canvas for the interplay of orange, ginger, and blueberry flavors. The blueberry vinegar perfumes the flesh of the roughy with just the right combination of sweetness and tartness.

¼ pound butter, at room
temperature
1 teaspoon finely minced
orange zest
½ teaspoon grated fresh
ginger
5 or 6 drops orange
flower water
1 tablespoon low-acid
(4.5 percent) blueberry
vinegar

1 medium bulb fennel
⅛ pound snow peas
1 small red onion
4 fillets orange roughy
¼ cup fresh blueberries
Salt and pepper
1 teaspoon finely
julienned orange zest
4 thin slices orange, 4
snow peas, a few blue-
berries for garnish

Make a compound butter by cutting the butter into chunks
and placing it in a food processor. Add the minced orange
zest and ginger. Mix together the orange flower water and
blueberry vinegar and add 1 teaspoon of the mixture to the
butter. Process until the ingredients are well combined and
smooth. Set the butter aside.

Trim the fennel, removing the large core, cut it into
thin slices, and set it aside. Trim the stem ends off the snow
peas and cut them into a thin julienne. Peel and trim the
onion and thinly slice. Toss the vegetables together.

Place the sheets of parchment on your working surface
and, in the center of each sheet, place about ¾ cup of the
vegetables, spread out as a bed for the fish. Add a little salt
and pepper and place a fillet of orange roughy on top. Top
the fish with a teaspoon of the compound butter, several
fresh blueberries, a little salt and pepper, and a sprinkling of
the julienned orange zest. Add a teaspoon of the blueberry
vinegar mixture. Fold the package as described on page 124.
Repeat the process until you have made 4 packets.

Place the packets on a baking sheet in a preheated 400°F. oven for 8 minutes. Remove them from the oven and transfer them to individual serving plates that have been garnished with a slice of orange, a snow pea, and a few blueberries. Serve immediately.

Chicken au Vinaigre

Serves 4

This voluptuously rich-tasting dish has ancient roots in the Loire Valley of France, where sultry hot summers guaranteed that some of the region's wine would inevitably turn to vinegar. An industrious people, the local

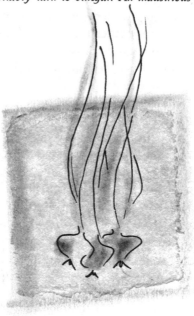

inhabitants transformed the loss into a delicious cuisine, and eventually, the town of Orleans at the northernmost point of the valley became known as the vinegar capital of the world. In spite of the seemingly large quantity of vinegar called for, this version of the ancient dish is only mildly tart. The traditional accompaniment is a green salad tossed with walnut oil and white wine vinegar for contrast; I frequently serve it with risotto, rice, or homemade potato gnocchi, and a simple green vegetable, such as steamed spinach or young green beans tossed with a bit of butter or olive oil.

1 whole roasting chicken, weighing about 3½ pounds

Salt and pepper

4 tablespoons butter

6 cloves garlic, unpeeled

4 tablespoons snipped chives

4 tablespoons Italian parsley, minced

¾ cup red wine vinegar (6 percent–7 percent acidity)

8 ounces hearty duck or veal stock

2 tablespoons tomato paste or sun-dried tomato paste

¼ to ½ cup heavy cream

Sprigs of Italian parsley and chives

Cut the chicken into pieces: breast-wing; thigh-leg. Rinse and dry the chicken and rub it with salt and pepper. Melt the butter in a large, heavy frying pan over medium heat and add the chicken, browning it until it is deep golden on both sides. Add the garlic and turn it frequently to brown it, but do not let it burn. Sprinkle 2 tablespoons each of the chives and parsley over the chicken, cover the pot, lower the heat, and let the chicken simmer gently for 20 minutes.

After 20 minutes, remove the chicken to a warm dish, cover, and place it in a warm oven. Turn the heat up under the frying pan and add the vinegar, scraping and deglazing the pan quickly. Add the stock and tomato paste. Stir constantly as the sauce reduces by one half. Press the pulp out of the garlic cloves with a fork, discard the skins, and blend the pulp into the sauce. Strain the sauce and return it to the pan. (You may hold the recipe at this point until all accompaniments are nearly done. Once you have added the cream to the sauce, it should be served promptly.)

Stir ¼ cup of the cream into the sauce and taste it. For a smoother, mellower sauce that is slightly less tart, add the remaining cream. Do not let the sauce boil again. Taste and adjust the seasonings and add the remaining chopped herbs. Return the chicken to the sauce, turning to coat it, and leave it on the heat for 10 minutes, making sure the sauce does not boil. Place the chicken on a serving platter, pour the sauce over it, and garnish with the sprigs of fresh herbs.

VEGETABLES

 # *Wilted Lettuce*

Serves 2

Here is an old recipe, a dish I remember my step-grandfather from Austria eating while everyone else at the table looked on. He never shared it and I never asked for a taste. He was something of a mystery to me and I would have been much too intimidated to intrude on his routine and request a taste of the strangely fragrant mound of wilted greens. The greens waited in a white oval bowl at his side and, after everyone else had come to the table, my grandmother would bring in the hot liquid from the stove and pour it over the lettuce. I have no way of knowing if this is how she made it, though the scent of this method is evocative of those early years.

3 slices bacon
1 tablespoon sugar
⅓ cup hearty, medium-
   acid red wine vinegar

4 cups shredded lettuce
   (I prefer red-leaf or
   Romaine)

Dice the bacon and sauté it until it is crisp. Add the sugar and the vinegar and heat until the sugar is dissolved and the mixture bubbling. Pour it over the lettuce, toss quickly, and serve immediately with some hot, crusty bread for soaking up any juices in the bottom of the dish.

VARIATION
After tossing the vinegar mixture with the lettuce, sprinkle 1 hard-boiled, sieved egg over the lettuce and add a sprinkling of fresh black pepper.

Radicchio in Vinegar

Serves 4 to 6

An updated version of Wilted Lettuce, this is a fragrant sidedish that I enjoy with Vinegar Eggs (page 123). It is also a perfect accompaniment to grilled or roasted meats. Cooking the radicchio mellows its characteristic bitterness considerably, and the vinegar adds a very pleasant tartness.

4 ounces bacon or
   pancetta, diced (see
   Note next page)
1 small red onion, diced
2 pounds radicchio

¼ cup black currant vine-
   gar, raspberry vinegar,
   or red wine vinegar (6
   percent acidity)
Salt and pepper

Fry the bacon or *pancetta* for 5 minutes, add the onion, and sauté the mixture for an additional 10 minutes over low to medium heat. Trim the *radicchio*, remove the root, and cut each head in quarters. Place the *radicchio* in the pan, one of the cut sides down. Sauté for 2 minutes and then turn the *radicchio* to the other cut side. Add half of the vinegar, cover the pan, and cook for 5 minutes.

Transfer the *radicchio* to a serving platter, add the remaining vinegar to the pan, turn the heat to high, and reduce the vinegar. Pour the juices, bacon, and onions over the *radicchio*, season with salt and pepper, and serve.

Note: If you use *pancetta*, you will need to use 2 tablespoons of olive oil in which to fry it.

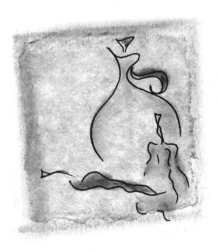

Roasted Peppers Balsamico

Roasting peppers draws out their natural sweetness in a way that other forms of cooking do not. Because they have a great deal of natural oiliness, they can be dressed with just a healthy splash of good vinegar. They are an excellent accompaniment to roast meats and poultry and are ideal served with the Baked Eggplant with Lamb (page 105). They also make good picnic food because they travel well and improve as they marinate in the vinegar.

6 fresh peppers, red, yellow, or green, or a combination
⅓ cup balsamic vinegar or medium-acid red wine vinegar
Salt and freshly ground black pepper
2 teaspoons finely minced fresh herbs such as oregano, Italian parsley, marjoram, and thyme

Char the skins of the peppers by placing them on a hot grill, over hot coals, directly over a gas flame, or under a broiler. Turn until the entire surface of each pepper is charred, but do not leave them on the heat so long that they cook through. It is best to begin with very cold peppers. After they are charred, place them in a paper bag or in a large bowl, covered, to steam and cool. After about 20 minutes, when the peppers are cool enough to handle, remove the charred skins, stems, and seeds. Do not rinse them in water or you will wash away the flavorful natural oils and juices.

Cut the peppers into ¼-inch-long strips—that is, a medium julienne—and place them in a nonreactive bowl. Add the vinegar, a pinch of salt, a sprinkle of pepper, and the fresh herbs.

VARIATION
Toss the peppers with 8 ounces of crumbled feta cheese and 6 cloves of thinly sliced garlic and serve over a small pasta, such as shells or *tripolini*.

CONDIMENTS

Peach & Currant Chutney
Makes approximately 2 quarts

Make this spicy chutney in midsummer or early fall, when there is an abundance of ripe peaches. Excellent with any curry dish, it is also delicious served with grilled chicken that has been marinated in balsamic vinegar. Homemade curries make wonderful gifts, so you might want to make a double batch to put up in half-pint jars for the holidays.

2 pounds dried currants
2 cups balsamic vinegar
4 cups apple cider vinegar
8 pounds peaches
2 pounds sugar
3 heads garlic, minced

¼ cup dried hot chilies
  (see Note below)
2-inch piece fresh ginger,
  peeled and minced
1 tablespoon salt

Note: For a less potent version, use half the quantity of dried chilies.

Place the currants in a large, nonreactive bowl or jar and add the balsamic vinegar and 2 cups of the apple cider vinegar. Let the mixture sit for several hours or overnight.

Heat a large pot of water to a boil. Place 3 or 4 peaches at a time in the water for 15 to 20 seconds. Remove them from the water, continue until all the peaches have been blanched, and peel the skin, which should be easy to remove. Slice the peaches lengthwise and place them in a large, heavy pot. Add the currants in the vinegar marinade and all the remaining ingredients. Heat thoroughly and, when the sugar has completely dissolved, taste the mixture. For a sweeter chutney, add more sugar; for a hotter chutney, add more dried chilies. Simmer over low heat, stirring occasionally, until the mixture is reduced by about a quarter to a third and thickens. Cooking time will be about 1 hour.

If you intend to use the chutney within a month, it may be kept in the refrigerator. To keep it longer, place it in sterilized pint or half-pint jars and process them in a water bath for 15 minutes.

Apricot Chutney

Makes approximately 6 pints

Apricots have a short season and you must make this delicious chutney before they vanish from the market. The best chutney is, of course, made from the finest raw materials, so look for apricots that taste like apricots, with lots of natural sweetness. This recipe appeared in my first book and reappears here because it is my favorite chutney. I serve it most often with roast pork loin. A batch made in the summer should last until the next apricot season, unless you give it all away at Christmas.

5 pounds ripe apricots, halved and stoned
3 pounds sugar
1 pound currants
3 heads garlic, cloves separated, peeled, and chopped
5 jalapeño chili peppers, seeded and cut into a very thin julienne
5 ounces fresh ginger, peeled and grated or chopped
1 ounce dried hot chilies (see Note below)
3 cups apple cider vinegar
1 to 2 tablespoons salt

Note: For a less potent version, use half the quantity of dried chilies.

In a large, heavy pot combine the apricots and sugar over medium heat. Stir continuously until the sugar is dissolved. Add all other ingredients, stir well, and simmer over low heat for 1 hour. Pour the chutney into hot sterilized pint or half-pint jars and process in a water bath for 15 minutes.

Persimmon Chutney

Makes about 6 pints

This has been my most popular chutney. A local mushroom grower likes it so much that he trades me his rare and luscious black chanterelles for jars of my persimmon chutney, an exchange that guarantees that I will continue to make chutney year after year. I particularly enjoy this condiment with grilled spicy sausages and polenta.

5 pounds soft-ripe persimmons	5 ounces fresh ginger, peeled and grated or chopped
2 pounds sugar or more to taste	½ ounce dried hot chilies (see Note below)
1 ½ pounds golden raisins	3 cups apple cider vinegar
3 heads garlic, cloves separated, peeled, and chopped	1 to 2 tablespoons salt

Note: Increase or decrease the chilies according to the intensity of heat desired; ½ an ounce will provide only moderate fire.

Remove the stem ends of the persimmons and cut them in half. Scoop out the few seeds in the center and remove the pulp from the skin with a spoon. Discard the skins, seeds, and stems. Place the persimmon pulp and 2 pounds of sugar in a heavy pot over a low flame. Stir until the sugar has dissolved. Taste the mixture and add more sugar if necessary to make a fairly sweet mixture. Add the remaining ingredients and taste again. If the balance of flavors seems right, simmer the mixture for about 1 hour. If not, add a little sugar for more sweetness or a little vinegar for more tartness.

After the mixture has simmered for 1 hour, ladle it into hot sterilized half-pint or pint jars and process in a water bath for 15 minutes.

Cranberry Chutney

Makes approximately 4 pints

Cranberry chutney has a deep, rich flavor that is an ideal accompaniment to all types of wild fowl and farm-raised dark-meat poultry. Of course, it is wonderful with turkey, but even better with duck, and divine with any smoked poultry. It will make a welcome addition to your Thanksgiving table.

8 cups cranberries	2 cups cider vinegar
8 cloves garlic, minced	2-inch piece fresh ginger,
2 onions, cut in small dice	peeled and minced
2 or 3 serrano or jalapeño	1 teaspoon each ground
chili peppers, stemmed,	cardamom, cloves,
seeded, and minced	cayenne pepper, and
2 cups currants	allspice
2 to 2½ cups granulated	3 pears, peeled, cored,
sugar	and minced

Rinse the cranberries under cool water and pick through them, discarding any that are soft or brown. Finely chop the cranberries in a food processor and place them in a large, nonreactive pot, along with the garlic, onions, peppers, currants, 1½ cups of the sugar, 1 cup of the vinegar, the ginger, and spices. Simmer over a medium flame, stirring frequently, until the mixture is very thick, about 20 minutes. Taste the chutney and add more sugar or more vinegar to adjust the balance between sweet and acid, add the pears, and simmer for an additional 10 minutes.

Remove from the heat and ladle into sterilized half-pint jars. Seal the jars, cool, and store until ready to use.

 *Peach Ketchup*

Makes 5 to 6 cups

For a commercial product to be legally named ketchup in the United States, it must contain tomatoes, vinegar, sugar, and spices. Similar condiments with no sugar must be labeled "imitation." It is an interesting evolution for a recipe in which the early colonists used tomatoes when they could not get the ingredients they had used in Europe, where ketchup was made with a variety of fruits and nuts. The inspiration for this recipe comes from a delightful little book, The Art of Accompaniment, *by Jeffree Sapp Brooks. I have altered it somewhat, as most cooks are wont to do. Try it with Perfect French Fries (page 101) or as a condiment for grilled chicken.*

5 pounds ripe peaches, peeled, pitted, and coarsely chopped
2½ cups unfiltered apple cider vinegar or peach vinegar (5 percent acidity)
1 teaspoon salt
1 pound brown sugar
1 small vanilla bean
Zest of 1 small orange
2 teaspoons mustard seed

1 cinnamon stick, 2 inches long
2-inch piece fresh ginger, peeled and sliced
1 teaspoon whole cloves
1 teaspoon whole allspice berries
1 nutmeg, cracked (use a mortar and pestle or a hammer)
1 teaspoon juniper berries

Combine the chopped peaches, vinegar, salt, and brown sugar in a large nonreactive pot. Add the remaining ingredients tied in several layers of cheesecloth. Bring the ingredients to a boil, reduce the heat, cover, and simmer until the peaches are very soft, approximately 30 minutes.

With a slotted spoon, transfer the peaches to a blender or food processor and purée them. Return the puréed peaches to the pot with the cooking liquid and spices. Simmer the mixture, uncovered, until it is very thick—about 1 hour—skimming off any foam as it forms on the top of the mixture.

Remove the bag of spices and ladle the ketchup into 5 or 6 sterilized, hot half-pint jars. Wipe the rims and cap immediately with hot lids and rings. Process in a boiling water bath for 15 minutes. Store in a cool, dark cupboard until ready to use. Refrigerate after opening.

Pickled Onions & Grapes

Makes 8 to 10 pints

Stanley Eichelbaum, a food writer and chef in San Francisco, loves this condiment and recommends that it be served with grilled fish or poultry; I serve it most often as part of an antipasti platter. Both the grapes and the onions are excellent with smoked salmon, on sandwiches, or accompanying grilled or roasted meats, poultry, or seafood.

MARINADE

3 ½ cups raspberry vinegar (up to 6 percent acidity)

3 ½ cups red wine

1 ⅓ cups sugar, or more to taste

Several gratings of whole nutmeg

10 whole allspice berries, crushed

10 whole cloves, crushed

1-inch piece cinnamon

8 to 10 cardamom seeds

Salt and pepper

3 pounds red onions, torpedos, if available

2 pounds organic, seedless Red Flame grapes

Place all of the ingredients for the marinade in a heavy, non-reactive saucepan, heat the mixture, and stir it until the sugar is melted. Taste and add more sugar if a sweeter marinade is desired. Set aside to cool.

Peel the onions and slice them very thin. Remove the grapes from their stems, rinse, and dry. Place the grapes and onions in pint or quart jars and cover with the marinade. I put both onions and grapes together in each jar and enjoy the subtle interplay of flavors the combination offers. For best results, let the ingredients rest in the marinade for at least 24 hours before using. The condiment will last for several weeks when stored in the refrigerator.

VARIATION
Use just onions or just grapes, doubling the quantities.

FLAVORED VINEGARS

Flavored vinegars fall into five general categories: fruit, herb, spice, vegetable, and blends. The first thing to recognize when making flavored vinegars is that the final product can be of no higher quality than the ingredients that go into it. Therefore, you must begin with a good-quality vinegar, one whose taste you already enjoy. I prefer a medium-acid vinegar (60 grain or 6 percent) and, for most fruit flavors, prefer one made with champagne grapes because the vinegar generally has a smooth taste, mild enough to allow the essential flavors of the fruit to shine through. Distilled vinegar is simply too harsh for making flavored vinegars. Cider and malt vinegars have their own distinctive flavor, making them suitable for some flavoring agents but not with others. Higher-acid vinegars or red wine vinegars are suitable for spice blends, but will eclipse the more delicate flavors of most fruits and herbs. Good red wine vinegars have a great deal of character on their own and those qualities should be encouraged either by featuring their natural flavor in certain dishes or by adding spices and herbs that enhance that specific natural goodness. When trying to capture the essence of fresh fruit at its peak of ripeness, why offer competition with a strongly flavored vinegar?

When working with vinegars in any capacity, it is essential to keep in mind their corrosive nature. That means that no metal utensils should be used. Strainers and funnels should be made of plastic, all containers should be of glass or porcelain, and lids of cork or plastic. Stir your vinegars with a wooden spoon. Stainless steel and food-grade plastic do not pose a problem, but I believe it is best to get in the habit of using all nonmetal materials when working with vinegar and using glass when storing it. Used wine bottles, especially tenths, are perfect for bottling your flavored vinegars.

Flavored vinegars make wonderful condiments for sprinkling on fresh fruit, steamed vegetables, soups, or stews. They can also be used in any recipe calling for vinegar; just be sure to use flavors that are compatible with the other ingredients in the dish or meal. For example, to accompany a traditional spaghetti with tomato sauce dinner, you might dress a green salad with an oregano vinegar. Use basil vinegar with fresh tomatoes. Chive vinegar is wonderful with cucumbers, as is lemon-thyme vinegar. Consider a mayonnaise made with fruit vinegar to accompany a fruit salad.

Fruit Vinegars

Makes about 2½ to 3 cups

The quantities given here yield a vinegar with a rich and voluptuous taste of fruit. I prefer to make my fruit-flavored vinegars this intense and then dilute them with some unflavored vinegar if a recipe requires more

*subtlety. Mostly, I just enjoy them as they are. My favorite is Cran-
berry Vinegar, which I make in large quantities every fall.*

4 cups chopped fruit   **2 cups vinegar (up to 6
                                      percent acidity)**

Place the chopped fruit in a glass jar or crock and pour the
vinegar over it. You should have just enough vinegar to
cover the fruit; add more if necessary. Store the mixture,
covered, in a cool pantry or the refrigerator for at least 2
days or up to 10 days, tasting frequently to determine when
your vinegar is sufficiently flavored. Strain the mixture
through several layers of cheesecloth or through a paper or
cloth coffee filter until the liquid is absolutely clear, pressing the fruit to remove all of the liquid. Bottle, close with a
cork, and store in a cool, dark cupboard.

Suggested Combinations

Berries (cranberry, raspberry, blackberry, boysen-
berry, or blueberry) with white wine or champagne
vinegar;
Golden raspberry with apple cider vinegar;
Pears, cored, with champagne vinegar;
Peaches, apricots, nectarines, pits removed, and persimmons with apple cider vinegar;
Oranges, lemons, and limes: use the juice and zest of
4 fruits, being careful not to include the bitter white
pith, with white wine or champagne vinegar;
Papaya, mango, and pineapple with unseasoned rice
vinegar (5 percent acidity) or apple cider vinegar

 *Garlic Vinegar*

Makes 4 cups

*Garlic vinegar is a staple in many pantries and often is used as the basis
for herb or spice vinegars. It can be made with either red wine vinegar or
white wine vinegar, and you might consider making both. Use the vinegar wherever the flavor of garlic will enhance a dish, and try it as a condiment in soups and stews, and on pizza.*

1 head garlic

**4 cups red or white wine
vinegar, of any strength**

Separate the cloves of garlic, discard the root, and cut the
cloves in half. You need not peel them. Place the cloves in
a glass jar or crock, pour the vinegar over them, and close
the container with a cork. Let the vinegar sit in a cool, dark

cupboard for a week before using it. Use the vinegar directly from the container, and replenish it as you use it. It should continue to provide lusty garlicky vinegar for about 6 months.

 Herb Vinegars

Makes 3 cups

My favorite herb vinegar is rosemary made with a rich red wine vinegar. It is the only one I use regularly, preferring to add other herbs fresh to specific dishes. You should experiment until you find your favorite combinations.

1 cup fresh herbs
3 cups vinegar (6 percent acidity)

Sprigs of fresh herbs, with their flowers, if available (when bottling)

Crush the fresh herbs, place them in a glass jar or crock, and cover with the vinegar. Let the mixture steep in a cool pantry for up to 1 month, tasting to determine when your vinegar is sufficiently flavored. Strain through cheesecloth or a coffee filter. Bottle, add a fresh sprig of the herb, and close with a cork. Store in a cool, dark cupboard.

Suggested Combinations

Rosemary with red wine vinegar
Chives with white wine vinegar
Sage with red or white wine vinegar
Oregano with red or white wine vinegar

Savory with white wine vinegar
Marjoram with red wine vinegar
Tarragon with champagne vinegar
Thyme with champagne vinegar

Peppercorn Vinegar

Makes 3 cups

Because pepper is such a universal seasoning, it goes perfectly well with any vinegar.

**3 tablespoons pepper-
corns, black or a mix-
ture of black, white,
and pink**

**3 cups vinegar; red wine,
white wine, or cham-
pagne are recommended**

Combine the ingredients in a glass jar, close with a nonmetallic lid, and store in a cool cupboard for 2 to 3 months. Strain the mixture through cheesecloth or a coffee filter into clean bottles, add a few fresh peppercorns, and close with a cork.

Ginger Vinegar

Makes 3 cups

This vinegar is a welcome addition wherever a recipe calls for rice vinegar. The two flavors are extremely complimentary, and it would be excellent in the Thai Vinaigrette (page 222).

1 large piece ginger root, about 3 inches long	3 cups rice vinegar (5 percent acidity)

Peel the ginger, slice it, and chop it coarsely. Place it in a glass jar or crock, cover it with the vinegar, and let it steep for 2 or 3 weeks. Taste it after the first week and thereafter until it has the desired aroma and taste of ginger. Strain the mixture through cheesecloth or a coffee filter and bottle it, closing the bottle with a cork.

 *Spice Vinegar*

Makes 4 cups

Some cooks recommend heating the vinegar and its flavoring agent before setting the mixture aside to steep. In general, I do not recommend this and feel that it can alter the flavor of both the vinegar and the flavoring. This spice vinegar can, however, be hurried along a little if you heat it slightly after the spices have been added. The heat helps release the flavor of the dried spices and, if you are sure to keep the temperature below 160°F., there should be no breakdown in the flavor of the vinegar or the spices.

1 tablespoon each whole cloves, allspice, and black peppercorns	1 whole nutmeg, cracked
2-inch piece cinnamon	1 teaspoon juniper berries
1 teaspoon cardamom seeds	4 cups red wine vinegar (up to 6½ percent acidity)

Place all of the ingredients, heated or not, in a crock or glass jar, cover, and set the mixture aside to steep for a month. Strain the vinegar into glass bottles, cork the bottles, and store them in a cool, dark cupboard.

Rose Petal Vinegar

Makes 3 cups

This is an almost heartbreakingly delicate vinegar, full of transporting aromas. Sprinkle it on fresh melons or use it in a subtle, fragrant mayonnaise or a hazelnut vinaigrette. Because it is so beautiful, it also makes a lovely gift. Remember, the deeper the color of the rose petals you use, the more vibrantly colored your vinegar.

4 cups rose petals, lightly crushed (see Note below)

3 cups champagne vinegar (6 percent acidity)

10 drops rosewater (optional; when bottling)

1 perfect rosebud (when bottling)

Note: The roses must be organic; absolutely free of any form of pesticide.

Combine the rose petals and the vinegar in a glass jar or crock, cover, and let the mixture sit in a cool pantry for up to 4 weeks. Taste the vinegar regularly and strain it when it is fragrant with the scent of the roses. Add the rosewater and bottle the vinegar, placing the rosebud in the bottle. Cork the bottle and store it in a cool, dark cupboard.

Cucumber-Dill Vinegar

Makes about 2½ to 3 cups

Cool and refreshing, this vinegar is wonderful with seafood salads, either in a vinaigrette or in a mayonnaise.

4 cups cucumber, peeled and chopped (see Note below)

1 teaspoon dill seed

2 cups champagne vinegar (6 percent acidity)

Sprigs of young dill weed

Note: If you have a garden or access to noncommercial cucumbers, you do not have to peel them. Commercial cucumbers, however, are frequently waxed and must be peeled.

Place the chopped cucumber and dill seed in a glass jar or crock and pour the vinegar over it. Store the mixture in a cool pantry or refrigerator for up to 3 weeks, tasting occasionally to determine when your vinegar is sufficiently flavored. Strain the mixture through several layers of cheesecloth and through a paper or cloth coffee filter until the liquid is clear, pressing the cucumber to remove all of the liquid. Bottle and insert a small sprig of fresh dill into the bottle. Close the bottle with a cork and store it in a cool, dark cupboard.

Complex Vinegars

Quite obviously, you could take this topic, and hence the possible recipes, to an extreme, coming up with as many combinations of flavors as there

*are ingredients available. I offer my favorite combinations here and rec-
ommend that you make them in small quantities until you discover a
favorite.*

Lemon Thyme Vinegar

Makes 3 cups

1 cup lemon thyme
3 cups lemon vinegar

Sprigs of lemon thyme
(when bottling)

Garlic and Rosemary Vinegar

Makes 3 cups

3 cloves garlic, peeled and
mashed

3 cups rosemary vinegar

Tropical Ginger Vinegar

Makes 3 cups

1 large piece ginger root,
about 3 inches long

3 cups mango, papaya, or
pineapple vinegar

Place the flavoring agent in a glass jar or crock and pour the
flavored vinegar over it. Let the mixture steep in a cool pantry for up to a month, tasting it at frequent intervals. The
garlic and rosemary vinegar is likely to be strong enough in
a week.

Strain the mixture and bottle the vinegar when it has
the intensity of flavor you want. Cork the bottles and store
them in a cool cupboard.

SAUCES

MIGNONETTE SAUCES

"A loaf of bread," the Walrus said,
*   "is what we chiefly need:*
Pepper and vinegar besides
*   Are very good indeed—*
Now if you're ready, Oysters dear,
*   We can begin to feed."*

Lewis Carroll,
Through the Looking-Glass

Ice-cold oysters on the half shell are among the simplest, purest gastronomic joys in the world and they require nothing more than a squeeze of lemon. They are also exquisite dressed up just a bit in a fancy Mignonette Sauce, a mixture of vinegar, shallots, salt, pepper, and the addition of another acid, wine, perhaps, or lemon juice. The numerous variations I use tie the oysters to the rest of the menu or to the celebration at hand—oysters are frequently part of a festive menu. The clear, bright taste of a good vinegar makes a perfect companion to plump shellfish.

Cranberry Mignonette

For a Christmas Eve dinner or a New Year's brunch, try this wintery mignonette.

3 tablespoons fresh cranberries, finely chopped
½ teaspoon orange zest, very finely minced
1 small shallot, minced

¾ cup cranberry vinegar (see Fruit Vinegars, page 145)
Juice of half an orange
½ teaspoon salt
1 teaspoon black pepper

Combine all of the ingredients and chill the mixture. Serve the sauce ice cold over freshly shucked oysters on the half shell.

Black Raspberry Mignonette

The slight sweetness of raspberry vinegar is a pleasing companion to the natural sweetness of oysters.

1 cup low-acid black raspberry vinegar
1 shallot, minced

Juice of 1 lemon
Salt and pepper

Mix the vinegar, shallot, and lemon juice together. Add a small amount of salt and pepper and chill. Serve over chilled oysters on the half shell.

Rice Vinegar Mignonette

The combination of ingredients in this spicy sauce is absolutely seductive. Make sure you have plenty of oysters on hand and be sure that the sauce is well chilled.

1 cup rice vinegar, unseasoned
Juice of 2 limes
1 shallot, finely chopped
1 serrano chili pepper,
   very finely chopped

¼ to ½ teaspoon fresh
   ginger, minced
2 tablespoons chopped
   cilantro leaves
¼ teaspoon salt

Combine the vinegar, lime juice, shallot, and *serrano* pepper. Place ¼ teaspoon ginger in a garlic press and press it firmly to release its juice into the vinegar mixture. Add the cilantro leaves and salt and taste the sauce. For a more pronounced ginger flavor, add another ¼ teaspoon. Chill the mignonette and serve it over ice-cold oysters on the half shell.

Beurre Blanc

Makes approximately 1 cup

The classic sauce beurre blanc, *which means literally "white butter," demonstrates the way in which acids—quite frequently, vinegar—play an essential role in classical cuisine. Beurre rouge is so named for the rosy hue added by the use of red wine and red vinegar. The sauce is an uncomplicated emulsion of butter in a very concentrated reduction of acids and shallots. There are many variations of this classic sauce, and endless arguments about the proper method. If it is to be served with seafood,* fish fumet *is often used in place of the vinegar. Some versions call for the addition of a small quantity of cream, others for a large quantity. It is important to be comfortable with the basic procedure before attempting variations.*

Beurre blanc *is heavenly with lobster and is an ideal sauce for any poached or broiled fish, for lighter meats such as veal and chicken, and for elegant vegetables such as asparagus. Beurre rouge can be served with grilled meats, poached eggs, salmon, swordfish, and shark.*

½ cup good dry white
  wine
⅓ cup medium-acid (5–6
  percent) white wine or
  champagne vinegar
2 tablespoons shallots,
  chopped very fine

¼ teaspoon salt
¼ teaspoon white
  pepper
½ pound unsalted butter,
  at room temperature

In a heavy saucepan, mix the wine, vinegar, shallots, and salt together and reduce over high heat to 3 tablespoons. Remove from the heat to cool and lower the flame to nearly just a flicker. The acid base must not evaporate, and the butter must not rise above about 130 degrees F. Return the pot to the heat, add the pepper, and whisk in the butter, tablespoon by tablespoon, until you have a creamy, smooth sauce. Strain the sauce directly over the food to be sauced or into a warm sauceboat. Serve immediately.

VARIATION
BEURRE ROUGE
½ cup red wine, such as
  Burgundy
⅓ cup medium-acid (5–6
  percent) red wine
  vinegar
2 tablespoons shallots,
  chopped very fine

¼ teaspoon salt
¼ teaspoon white
  pepper
½ pound unsalted butter,
  at room temperature

Prepare the sauce following the directions for *Beurre blanc.*

Hollandaise

Delicious, caloric, laden with cholesterol, hollandaise is the mother sauce of all warm emulsions. Once the basic technique is understood, endless creative variations are possible. The mother sauce uses neither of our subject ingredients—not oil, not vinegar—but delicious changes can be made by replacing the traditional lemon juice with vinegar. Because of concerns about health, these sauces are used less often than they once were. They are, however, exquisitely delicious, and I do not agree with cooks who attempt to create healthy facsimiles. There are none. Rather than eat a fraudulent copy of a true hollandaise, indulge in the real thing on special occasions.

Blender Hollandaise

Makes about 1 cup

½ cup butter
3 egg yolks
1 tablespoon hot water

2 tablespoons lemon juice
¼ teaspoon salt
Pinch cayenne pepper

Melt the butter until it is foamy. While it is melting, place the egg yolks, hot water, lemon juice, salt, and cayenne into the blender. When butter is ready, remove it from the heat. Process the egg yolk mixture for 30 seconds. Slowly drizzle in the butter, continuing to process the entire time. If you will not be serving the sauce immediately, hold it by placing the blender container in a bowl of medium-hot water, at between 140° and 150°F. Hollandaise sauce must never reach a temperature of 180°F. or above or the emulsion will break.

VARIATIONS

RASPBERRY HOLLANDAISE Use 2 tablespoons raspberry vinegar (4.5 percent acidity), 1 teaspoon fresh lemon juice, and a pinch of sugar instead of the cayenne.

HOLLANDAISE DIJON Add 1 tablespoon Dijon mustard, omit the lemon juice and cayenne, and add 1 tablespoon champagne vinegar and a pinch of white pepper.

ANCHOVY HOLLANDAISE Omit the lemon juice and salt and replace them with vinegar from Anchovies in Vinegar (page 118) and 1 teaspoon anchovy paste or one anchovy fillet, finely chopped and added with the egg yolks. Use more anchovies to taste, but no more than 3.

DESSERTS

Vinegar Taffy

Makes about ½ pound

Making candy is fun, and this variation on traditional taffy is delicious, too. Once made, the pieces should be wrapped and stored in a tin.

1 ¼ cup sugar
¼ cup balsamic vinegar
2 teaspoons butter

1 teaspoon pure vanilla
  extract

In a heavy saucepan, heat the sugar, vinegar, and butter over low heat, stirring until the sugar is dissolved. Increase the heat and bring the mixture to 265°F. Pour the candy onto a marble slab or buttered platter and let it cool.

Have a working surface—preferably of marble—sprinkled with confectioner's sugar and have a pair of kitchen shears well buttered. When the candy will hold a dent when pressed with a finger, sprinkle the vanilla over it and, with greased fingers, gather it up into a ball. Be certain that the entire mass has cooled sufficiently too handle or you could receive a nasty burn. Pull the taffy, using both hands to stretch it and fold it over. This process will work best if you establish a steady, rhythmic movement, stretching your hands about 18 inches apart, quickly folding the taffy back on itself, and repeating until the mass becomes a shiny, glistening ribbon.

Quickly gather the mass up into your hands. Stretch it into thin ropes, make cuts every inch, and let the pieces fall onto the sugared surface. Place the candy in a tightly covered container.

VARIATIONS

Try this taffy with fruit vinegars. My favorite combinations include:

> Blueberry vinegar and ¼ teaspoon clove extract
> Raspberry vinegar and ¼ teaspoon lemon extract
> Cranberry vinegar and ¼ teaspoon orange extract

 # Gelato Modena

Makes approximately 1 quart

This is probably my favorite recipe in the book. It is so simple, yet results in a surprisingly rich and complex taste on the palate. I also love serving it because no one can ever figure out what is in it. Pears, they've insisted, or apples. Never does anyone guess vinegar. The only person who has ever figured it out is my daughter Gina, whose approach to food is uncompli- cated and absolutely without pretension. "Try this new dessert," I urged.

"What do you want me to try that for?" she responded. "It's vinegar."

You cannot and should not use aceto balsamico tradizionale *in this recipe. Even if you could find some, it would be ridiculously ex- pensive and a waste of that rare condiment. If you find yourself, however, in happy possession of some of the real thing, you might sprinkle a few drops over this delicious ice just before serving it. I recommend serving this gelato with sliced strawberries or whole* fraises de bois *that have been tossed with a little of the same vinegar used in the gelato and some freshly cracked black pepper.*

3 cups water	1 to 2 teaspoons fresh
1 ½ cups sugar	ground black pepper
⅔ cup balsamic vinegar	¼ cup heavy cream
1 teaspoon vanilla extract	

Combine the water and sugar in a heavy, nonreactive pan and bring to a boil. Cover the pan and simmer the mixture for 5 minutes. Remove the pan from the heat, stir in the vin- egar, vanilla, and pepper. Cool the mixture to room temperature, then chill it for 2 hours in the refrigerator before freezing it in an ice-cream freezer according to the manufacturer's instructions. Just before freezing, add the cream to the sugar mixture. Transfer the *gelato* to a container and chill it overnight before serving.

VARIATION
Omit the cream. The *gelato* will be slightly sharper and more intense, and lack a bit of the depth of the other version. It is, however, delicious, and I recommend it for anyone concerned about the intake of dairy fats.

 *Vinegar Pie*

Serves 6 to 8

Vinegar pie is an old American tradition, developed for times when other flavoring ingredients—fresh fruit and natural juices, for example—were unavailable. I include it here in part for its historical interest, in part because it is delicious. You might consider experimenting with the vinegars and extracts. Combine blueberry vinegar with clove extract or cranberry vinegar with orange extract, a tablespoon of orange zest, and walnuts instead of pecans. The crust is excellent for other pies, too, being light and flaky, with just a spark of tartness.

PIE CRUST
1 ¼ cups all-purpose flour
Pinch salt
6 tablespoons unsalted
  butter, well chilled

2 tablespoons lard, well
  chilled
1 tablespoon cold apple
  cider vinegar
2 tablespoons ice water

163

FILLING

4 eggs	1 teaspoon vanilla extract
¾ cup granulated sugar	6 tablespoons unsalted butter
½ cup brown sugar	1 cup pecan halves, toasted
2 tablespoons vinegar such as balsamic, fruit, apple cider, or citrus-flavored	½ cup heavy cream, lightly whipped with a little sugar and vanilla

Place the flour and salt in a food processor with the metal blade. Add the butter and lard and pulse quickly several times, until the mixture is evenly blended. Add the vinegar and the water, pulse 3 or 4 times, and turn the dough out onto plastic wrap. Press the dough together quickly with your hands, wrap it, and refrigerate it for an hour.

Roll out the dough either between 2 sheets of parchment or wax paper or on a pastry cloth. Transfer the rolled pie dough to a 9-inch pie pan and trim the edges. Line the dough with a sheet of parchment and fill it with beans or pie weights. Refrigerate the shell for 30 minutes and preheat the oven to 450°F. Bake the pie shell for 10 minutes and remove the weights and paper lining. Return the pie shell to the oven, lower the heat to 350°F., and bake until the pastry is just barely golden, about 8 to 10 minutes. Remove the pie shell from the oven and let it cool.

Beat the eggs until they are smooth and creamy. Add the sugar, vinegar, and vanilla and beat everything together well. Melt the butter, let it cool just slightly, and beat it into the egg mixture. Spread the pecans over the surface of the pie shell and pour the egg mixture over them. Bake at 350°F. for about 25 minutes. Remove the pie from the oven and let cool for 15 minutes before serving it with freshly whipped cream.

THE UNION OF OPPOSITES

AND NOW WE COME TO THE ESSENCE OF THE book, the marriage of oil and vinegar. Few pantry staples were meant for each other as thoroughly as these two ingredients are. Vinaigrettes, mayonnaise and other cold emulsions, and salsas all depend on the interplay of acid and oil. Our culinary possibilities expand tremendously when we become adept at choosing oil and vinegar companions and skilled at combining them. It is crucial to know your ingredients well, to taste them separately before combining them. A writer, a chef, can tell you that, say, sherry vinegar and toasted sesame oil do not work well together, but it is better to rely on your own experience than what someone has told you. Besides, not all chefs and writers agree. It is, ultimately, a matter of personal taste. Taste your oils, taste your vinegars before joining them together, and before long you will know automatically what works together in harmony and what competes unpleasantly.

I offer you here my favorite combinations, ways of joining together ingredients I have worked with for years, as well as some that I have recently discovered. I am always tasting, always discovering new ingredients and new kitchen companions. My best advice is that you continue to do the same.

Bread with Oil & Vinegar Pour olive oil into a plate or a shallow bowl. Add a small quantity of vinegar, about ⅓ as much vinegar as oil, season with salt and pepper, and serve with hot bread or rolls. Balsamic vinegar, sherry vinegar, and red wine vinegar are the best choices, and the crustier the bread, the better.

Asparagus with Raspberry Vinaigrette Serve steamed asparagus with black raspberry vinaigrette (page 216) and fresh raspberries as a first course or elegant side dish.

Rice & Vinegar Steamed rice with a little of your favorite vinaigrette is delicious and provides a healthy alternative to rice and butter.

Vinaigrette as a Marinade Use your favorite vinaigrette as a marinade, selecting lighter ones for chicken and seafood, heartier ones made with red wine vinegar for beef and lamb. Marinate the food for up to 1 hour before grilling.

Chicken Sandwiches Grill or broil a boneless chicken breast, place it on a hot French roll, and top it with two tablespoons of mustard vinaigrette and a handful of arugula or other fresh greens.

Chicken with Chutney Marinate pieces of chicken in olive oil and balsamic vinegar for 1 hour, grill or broil them, and serve with Peach and Currant Chutney (page 136).

APPETIZERS

Grilled Prawns
with *Honey Pepper Vinaigrette & Strawberries*

Makes 20 to 24 appetizers

The combination of flavors in this simple appetizer is heavenly, with just the right mix of sweetness, tartness, and heat from the pepper. It is also easy to make and can be increased for a large crowd.

1 pound raw prawns, 20
   to 24 per pound
Honey Pepper Vinaigrette
   (page 219)
2 to 3 tablespoons sherry

2 pints small, sweet strawberries
24 wooden skewers,
   soaked in water
Sprigs of mint leaves

Peel and devein the prawns. In a small, heavy skillet, heat about 3 tablespoons of the vinaigrette until it is fragrant. Sauté the prawns, a few at a time, very quickly, for about 2 minutes on each side. Remove the prawns to a holding platter, deglaze the pan with the sherry, and pour the juices over the prawns. Let the prawns sit until you are ready to serve, refrigerating them if they are to wait longer than 30 minutes.

Rinse and dry the strawberries and set aside 24 perfect berries. Arrange the remaining berries on a serving platter and chill until you are ready to use them.

Place each prawn on a wooden skewer. Cook the prawns quickly on a stove-top grill or over low coals on a barbecue. As you remove the prawns from the grill, quickly place one of the reserved strawberries onto each skewer. Arrange the prawns decoratively on top of the strawberries on the serving platter and spoon the vinaigrette over the prawns and strawberries. Garnish with sprigs of mint.

VARIATION

Thinly slice 1 large or 2 medium fresh fennel bulbs. Reserve the 24 perfect berries, slice the remaining strawberries, and toss them with the fennel and 2 tablespoons of the dressing. Place on a serving platter and top with the skewered grilled prawns and berries.

Onion Confit with Smoked Duck & Chutney

Serves 10 to 12 as an appetizer; 8 as a pizza

Red wine vinegar in this recipe adds a subtle dimension to the smoky sweetness of the onions. Served on baguettes or other hearty bread, this makes a delightful appetizer. If served as a pizza, it needs only a green salad as an accompaniment. The onion confit will keep refrigerated for several days.

Several tablespoons melted smoked duck fat or olive oil

3 pounds red onions, thinly sliced

¼ cup red wine vinegar (see Note below)

2 anchovies, finely chopped

Salt and pepper

1 smoked duck, fat removed and discarded

1 sourdough baguette or 2 pizza shells, each 8 to 10 inches in diameter

Cranberry Chutney (optional) (page 139)

Note: Use red wine vinegar that has been used to marinate anchovies.

In a heavy skillet, heat the duck fat or olive oil. Sauté the onions until they are limp and transparent. Add the vinegar, anchovies, and salt and pepper to taste. Combine the ingredients well and continue to sauté them until most of the liquid is reduced and the onions are very, very soft. Set the mixture aside to cool.

Remove the meat from the carcass of the duck and cut it into thin slices. To serve as an appetizer, lightly toast the bread and spread the cooled onion confit over the surface. Top each slice with a small amount of chutney, if you are using it. Serve with red wine.

To serve as a pizza, have the pizza dough ready and form 2 pizza shells. Divide the onion mixture between the 2 and spread it over the surface of each. Place the pizza on a pizza stone or greased baking sheet in a 475°F. oven for 10 minutes, until the crust is just starting to turn golden. Open the oven, quickly distribute the duck meat over the surface of the pizzas, and continue baking them for 5 minutes. Remove the pizzas from the oven and place them on a cutting surface. Cut each pizza into 8 slices and garnish each slice with a dollop of cranberry chutney. Serve immediately.

Marinated & Grilled Beef Heart
Anticuchos—from Peru & Bolivia
Serves 16 or more as an appetizer

South American Cooking *by Barbara Karoff offers a delicious culinary tour, full of inspiring recipes that I use regularly. This is one of my favorites, and a perfect demonstration of vinegar being used to make an inexpensive cut of meat more appealing. These little cubes of vinegary beef hearts are sold in Peru by street vendors and are eagerly devoured by* the local residents. A single beef heart is enormous and will make dozens of these little appetizers. As beef heart is also inexpensive, it makes a perfect appetizer for a large number of guests.

1 beef heart

MARINADE

6 to 8 cloves garlic, pressed
2 serrano or jalapeño chili peppers, seeded and minced
2 tablespoons ground cumin or cumin seeds, powdered

½ tablespoon dried oregano, crumbled
Salt and pepper to taste
1½ to 2 cups red wine vinegar
Wooden skewers, soaked in water

SAUCE

½ cup dried hontaka chili peppers or other dried hot chili peppers, seeded

1 teaspoon annatto powder (see Note below)
1 tablespoon safflower oil
Salt to taste

Note: If *annatto* powder is unavailable, substitute *achiote* paste, which is available in Latin markets.

Clean the beef heart thoroughly, removing all nerves and fat. Cut it into 1-inch cubes and place the cubes in a glass or stainless-steel bowl.

To make the marinade, combine the garlic, fresh chilies, cumin, oregano, salt and pepper, and 1½ cups of the vinegar. Pour this mixture over the meat. Add more vinegar, if necessary, to cover it completely. Marinate the meat in the refrigerator between 12 and 24 hours. Then, about 1 hour before grilling, remove the meat from the marinade and thread the cubes on skewers. Reserve the marinade.

For the sauce, pull the stems from the dried chilies, shake out the seeds, and soak the pods in warm water for 30 minutes. In a blender or food processor, combine the chilies with the *annatto* powder, oil, and salt. Add enough of the reserved marinade (about ¾ cup) to make a thick sauce.

Brush the skewered meat with the sauce and grill it over hot coals or under a broiler, turning and basting to cook the cubes quickly on all sides. The *anticuchos* are best cooked medium-well, about 3 or 4 minutes on the grill. Serve with the remaining sauce for dipping.

VARIATION

Cut the meat into lengthwise strips about 2 inches wide. Cut the strips, again lengthwise, into long slices about ⅛ inch thick. Thread the long, thin slices on wood skewers in an undulating fashion. Marinate the skewered meat for about 6 hours. It will cook to perfection very quickly, so watch it closely.

SOUPS

 *Smoky Gazpacho*

Serves 4

Few things refresh as much as a cool gazpacho *on a hot day, and this one brings a subtle smoky note to the crisp flavors and textures, making* Romesco *sauce the perfect accompaniment. For a dramatic appearance and more delicate taste, make this soup with golden tomatoes.*

1 medium red onion or 3 small red torpedo onions

2 sweet red peppers

6 large ripe tomatoes

6 cloves garlic, minced

2 small cucumbers, peeled, seeded, and diced

2 small zucchini, diced

1 cup chicken stock

½ cup extra virgin olive oil

3 tablespoons sherry vinegar or red wine vinegar

2 tablespoons chopped fresh herbs, such as marjoram, oregano, Italian parsley, chives, and thyme

Romesco Sauce (page 236)

Remove the root end and papery skin of the onions. Roast the onions and peppers on a grill or under a broiler, turning them often, until the skins of the peppers are charred and the onions are browned and partially cooked. Place the peppers in a paper bag until they have cooled, about 20 minutes. While the peppers are cooling, prepare the remaining vegetables. Plunge the tomatoes into rapidly boiling water for 10 seconds. Remove and plunge them into ice water. Dry the tomatoes, cut them in half, remove the seeds, and chop them coarsely. Chop the grilled onions. In a large bowl toss together the onions, garlic, cucumbers, zucchini, and all but ¾ cup of the tomatoes.

Remove the charred skins, stems, and seeds from the peppers. Cut one pepper into chunks and place it in a blender along with the reserved ¾ cup of tomatoes and the chicken stock. Process until the mixture is smooth. Strain through a sieve into the vegetables. Cut the remaining pepper into small dice and add it to the mixture, along with the olive oil, vinegar, and fresh herbs. Chill the soup for at least

2 hours before serving. Top each portion with a healthy spoonful of *Romesco* sauce.

Roasted Red Pepper Soup
with Toasted Coriander Cream

Serves 4 to 6

Roasted peppers provide one of the more delicious flavors of all vegetables. The transformation they go through between the raw and roasted states amazes me. This soup takes advantage of that rich roasted flavor, which is enhanced by the addition of the balsamic vinegar.

6 red bell peppers
Olive oil
1 medium yellow onion, diced
8 cloves garlic, minced
1 quart chicken stock
1 teaspoon ground cumin
2 teaspoons toasted coriander seed, crushed
1/8 to 1/4 cup balsamic vinegar

1/8 cup Madeira wine
Salt
1/2 cup crème fraîche or sour cream
3 tablespoons half-and-half
Juice of 1 lime
Pinch sugar
Pinch salt
Several sprigs cilantro

Roast the peppers until the skins are charred and set them aside to cool. Heat the olive oil in a heavy skillet, add the onion, and sauté it until it is soft and transparent. Add the garlic and sauté for another 2 minutes. Remove from the heat and set aside.

Remove the stems, seeds, and blackened skins from the peppers and cut them into chunks. Place the peppers and the onion mixture in a blender container along with 1 cup of the chicken stock. Blend until the mixture has been liquefied, adding more stock as needed to achieve the proper consistency. Pour the mixture into a heavy pot.

Add remaining chicken stock until the mixture is the proper consistency for a soup, neither too thick nor too thin. Add the cumin, 1 teaspoon of the coriander, ⅛ cup balsamic vinegar, and the Madeira. Taste the mixture and add salt and the remaining vinegar if necessary. The soup should be sweet and rich, with just a hint of tartness from the vinegar. Set the soup aside until you are ready to serve.

Mix together the *crème fraîche* or sour cream, half-and-half, remaining coriander, and lime juice. Add a pinch of sugar and a pinch of salt, taste the cream, and adjust the seasoning.

Heat the soup, ladle it into warm bowls, and top each serving with a generous spoonful of the coriander cream and several cilantro leaves.

Golden Beet Borscht

Serves 4

Delicate and subtle, this soup is an evocative starter to any meal and particularly delightful to one with Mediterranean or specifically Greek overtones. The yogurt mixture that crowns the golden liquid is a variation of the traditional tsatsíki, *a Greek yogurt and cucumber salad to which I have added chives.*

3 tablespoons vegetable oil, corn, olive, peanut, or canola (and more as needed)
1 medium yellow onion, diced
1 small carrot, diced
1 medium russet (baking) potato, diced
3 cups (approximately 1 pound) golden beets
1 teaspoon minced fresh ginger
1 teaspoon ground cumin
3 cups chicken, duck, or veal stock
$1/3$ cup apple cider vinegar or sherry wine vinegar
1 cucumber, peeled, seeded, and minced
Salt
3 cloves garlic, minced
3 tablespoons snipped chives and several uncut chives for garnish
8 ounces plain yogurt

Heat the vegetable oil in a heavy pan and add the diced onion. Sauté the onion until it is soft, about 5 minutes. Add the diced carrot, potatoes, beets, ginger, and $3/4$ teaspoon of the cumin. Use more oil if necessary. Sauté the vegetables, stirring frequently to ensure that they do not brown or burn, until the mixture is very soft. Add the stock and vinegar and simmer for 20 minutes.

While the soup is cooking, toss the chopped cucumber with about a teaspoon of salt and place it in a colander to drain for 20 minutes. Squeeze out any excess moisture. Toss together the cucumber, garlic, and snipped chives and stir in the yogurt. Set the mixture aside.

When the beet mixture has simmered for 20 minutes, purée it in a blender or food processor or with an immersion blender, and strain it through a sieve. Pour the soup into warmed bowls and place a heaping tablespoon of the yogurt mixture in the center of each. Dust each serving with a small amount of the remaining cumin and garnish with two or three chives. Serve immediately.

MAIN COURSES

Spaghetti with Chard & Pecans

Serves 4

This simple, rustic pasta offers a robust blend of flavors and textures. Serve it as a main course when you wish to eat simply, or as a first course in a more complex meal. If you are able to find white truffle oil, the variation suggested at the end of this recipe is an ideal way of using it. The aroma of truffles permeates the other ingredients, producing an altogether delightful effect.

4 to 6 ounces feta cheese
¾ cup pecan halves or pieces
¾ cup roasted sweet peppers, cut into medium julienne
2 tablespoons minced Italian parsley
1 bunch (about 1 pound) Swiss chard
¼ pound pancetta, diced

¾ pound dried pasta, spaghetti or spaghettini
¼ cup extra virgin olive oil
2 cloves garlic, peeled
3 tablespoons medium-acid red wine vinegar
Salt and freshly ground black pepper
1 cup homemade garlic croutons (page 88)

Have a large pot of salted, boiling water ready for the pasta. Cut the feta cheese into small cubes (½ an inch to a side or a little smaller) and place them in large bowl. Toast the pecans in a heavy, dry skillet, tossing them occasionally, until they brown, about 10 minutes. Cool the nuts slightly, add them to the cheese, along with the sweet peppers and parsley, and toss the mixture. Remove the large stems from the chard and wash and dry it well. Cut the leaves into medium-sized strips and set aside. Sauté the *pancetta* until it is just barely crisp and add it to the cheese mixture.

Cook the pasta according to the directions on the package. While the pasta is cooking, place the olive oil in a sauté pan, press the garlic into the oil, and add the chard. With the pan over medium heat, toss to coat the chard, add the vinegar, cover, and simmer briefly, until the chard is completely wilted. Drain the pasta, but do not rinse it in cold water. Add the chard to the feta cheese mixture and top with the pasta. Toss the mixture well and taste it. Add salt, pepper, and more a little more vinegar as desired. If the pasta seems too dry, drizzle on a little olive oil. Top with the croutons and serve immediately.

VARIATION
Use freshly grated Parmesan cheese in place of the feta cheese; omit the pecans; toss the pasta with 2 tablespoons white truffle oil immediately before serving.

Poached Trout with Fennel

Serves 4 as a main course; 8 as an appetizer

This is an elegant dish, suitable for a variety of occasions. It is a lovely prelude to a hearty but formal winter dinner and makes a great luncheon main course on a warm spring day. It is particularly convenient because the mayonnaise can be made and the trout poached a day before serving, leaving little to be done at the last minute.

4 medium rainbow trout
Court bouillon (see page 182)
3 small or 2 medium fennel bulbs
½ cup olive oil
2 tablespoons champagne vinegar
1 lemon

1 tablespoon fresh herbs, such as thyme, dill, Italian parsley, and marjoram
Salt and pepper
Herb Mayonnaise, page 232
Sprigs of fresh herbs for garnish

Poach the trout briefly, for about 8 minutes, in the court bouillon. Drain and, while the trout are still warm, separate each fillet from the skin, bones, and tail. Place the fillets in a flat dish, with parchment or foil between the layers. Chill until ready to use.

Remove any bruised, outer layers of the fennel, cut off the thick part of the root end, and slice the bulbs horizontally into ¼-inch strips. Mix together the oil, vinegar, juice of the lemon, herbs, salt, and pepper.

To serve, toss the fennel with the dressing and divide it among the serving plates. For a main luncheon course, on each plate arrange 2 trout fillets, partially draped over the fennel. For an appetizer course, use just 1 fillet. Top each piece of trout with a spoonful of herb mayonnaise, garnish with sprigs of herbs, and serve.

Poached Salmon
with Two Salsas

Serves 4

This sweet and delicate salmon dish is perfect for a summer brunch, luncheon, or light dinner. The slow poaching of the salmon guarantees that it will be as tender as butter, and the raspberry vinegar in the court bouillon perfumes the fish ever so slightly, adding an element that ties the fish to the flavors of the salsa.

Court bouillon (recipe follows), using raspberry vinegar instead of cider vinegar

4 steaks or fillets of wild salmon, 6 to 8 ounces each

½ recipe Mango Salsa, page 226

½ recipe Cherry & Corn Salsa, page 225

Sprigs of cilantro, mint, and thyme for garnish

Place the court bouillon, which should be at room temperature, in a poaching pan or large, nonreactive pot over low heat. Add the salmon to the liquid, arranging each piece so that it is surrounded by the liquid and not touching the other pieces of salmon. Using an instant-read thermometer as your guide, slowly allow the temperature of the liquid to rise to about 160°F. and hold it there for 10 minutes. Turn off the flame and let the salmon sit in the liquid for 20 minutes. (If you are using an electric stove, remove the pan from the burner.) Remove the salmon to drain on absorbent toweling. Serve the fish immediately or refrigerate it for 2 hours to serve it chilled.

To serve, place a piece of salmon on each of 4 serving plates. Add a healthy spoonful of each salsa, one on each side of the fish. Decorate the top of the salmon with a small quantity of each salsa. Garnish with the sprigs of fresh herbs.

Court Bouillon

A court bouillon is the traditional seasoned bath in which seafood is poached. In the classic court bouillon, a neutral flavored vinegar is used. Occasionally I will vary the vinegar to marry the poached fish to the sauce that will later dress it. If, for example, I am serving a salmon medallion with a raspberry hollandaise, I use a raspberry vinegar in the poaching liquid. The bath should be made in the poaching vessel, and the amount you need will depend on the size of the container. This recipe can easily be halved, doubled, or tripled.

1 quart water
½ bottle white wine (see Note next page)
½ cup cider vinegar
Half a lemon, cut in quarters, or the juice of 1 lemon
1 large carrot

2 large yellow onions, cut in quarters
1 medium leek, trimmed and cut into 2-inch lengths
3 sprigs Italian parsley
2 sprigs fresh thyme
1 bay leaf
1 tablespoon salt

Remove the rack from your poaching pan and add all of the ingredients. Bring the mixture to a boil, simmer for 30 minutes, and remove the pan from the heat until you are ready to use the court bouillon. When you poach your seafood, simply place it on the poaching rack and lower it into the bouillon. The vegetables will rest happily underneath.

After poaching, the liquid will be infused with fish protein and will spoil quickly. If you wish to reuse it, strain it as soon as it is cool enough to handle, and refrigerate or freeze it immediately. To reuse it, bring the bouillon to room temperature and extend it with more water, wine, vinegar, and vegetables, tasting it to achieve the proper balance of flavor.

Note: A crisp white wine such as a Sauvignon Blanc or dry Chardonnay is ideal, though the choice should be made with an eye to finance as well as taste. Never, ever use a sweet wine in a court bouillon. I also recommend that you avoid the use of red wine. Unless you use a very good red wine, and thus an expensive one, it will turn an unpleasant bluish color, staining your fish in the process. Given the price of good-quality red wine, it seems a waste to use it in this way.

Fillet of Sole
with Warm Tomato Vinaigrette

Serves 4

For anyone concerned with calories or fat, this is an ideal meal, low-fat, light, refreshing, and delicately delicious. Make it during tomato season for the best possible taste.

8 fillets of sole, 4 to 6 ounces each
Salt and pepper
2 tablespoons white wine vinegar
Half a lemon
Canola oil
Warm Tomato Vinaigrette (page 223)
Fresh herbs for garnish

Rinse the fillets of sole, pat them dry, and season them with salt and pepper. Bring 2 to 3 inches of water to boil in a pot with a steamer insert. Add the vinegar and the half lemon, cut in pieces. Brush the inside surface of the insert with a coating of canola oil. Place the fish on the surface of the insert, place over the boiling liquid, cover, and steam until the fish is just cooked through, about 5 minutes.

While the fish is cooking, place about 3 tablespoons of warm tomato vinaigrette on each of 4 plates. When the fish is done, place 2 fillets on each plate, and garnish the fish with another tablespoon of sauce and sprigs of fresh herbs. Serve immediately.

Chicken Vinaigrette Diane

Serves 4 to 6

The success of any chicken dish depends in large part on the quality of the chicken. I am lucky to live near the home of the first range chicken, Rocky, and that is what I use most of the time, although I occasionally use little game hens, cutting them in half for a light luncheon, or into smaller pieces to serve as appetizers. The ideal companions are Wild Rice Salad (page 206) and simple blanched green beans tossed with butter or walnut oil.

1 free-range chicken or 3 small game hens
Vinaigrette Diane (see page 221)
Salt and pepper
¾ cup currants
Balsamic vinegar

½ teaspoon vanilla extract
3 cups cooked wild rice (about 1 cup raw)
2 shallots, minced
¾ cup walnuts, toasted and coarsely chopped

Several hours before cooking, rinse the chicken thoroughly and pat it dry. Have the vinaigrette in a squeeze bottle. Using your finger, carefully separate the skin near the breast area from the flesh, but do not loosen it in the center. Squirt 2 or 3 tablespoons of the vinaigrette under the skin on each side of the chicken and then press on the skin to distribute the dressing. Salt and pepper the inside of the bird and squirt in 2 tablespoons or so of the dressing, covering the interior. Massage some dressing on the outer skin of the bird, place it in a plastic bag, and refrigerate it until 30 minutes before cooking time.

Soak the currants in just enough balsamic vinegar (to which you have added the vanilla) to cover them. Let them sit for 30 minutes and strain them, reserving the juices for another recipe, chutney, perhaps. Just before cooking, toss the wild rice, currants, shallots, and walnuts with 3 tablespoons of the dressing and place the mixture in the cavity of the bird. Tie the legs closed. Cover the breast of the bird loosely with foil and bake in a 425°F. oven for between 50 minutes and 1¼ hours. Remove the foil for the last 15 minutes and brush the bird liberally with additional vinaigrette.

VARIATION

Cut a game hen or guinea hen into small pieces: thigh with leg and breast with wing. Place the pieces in a shallow baking dish, pour the marinade over them, and turn them to coat them well. Marinate for several hours before cooking. To cook, grill over hot coals or on a stove-top grill, brushing with the sauce several times. Serve as an appetizer, or on a bed of wild rice as a light main course.

Grilled Beef with Chimichurra Marinade

Serves 6

This version of an increasingly popular marinade comes directly from its roots in Argentina from a friend's father, Carlos Rebagliati, who still lives in the country of his birth. When asked if parsley or cilantro should be added, he rebuffed the idea gruffly, "What do you need those things for? We've always done it like this. It is good." So don't mess with it! Marinate round steak or any sliced beef for a few hours, grill it quickly, and serve it with rice and the accompanying salsa.

3 pounds beef, round steak, top sirloin, or market steak, trimmed of fat and sliced
2 cups olive oil
1 cup red wine vinegar
1 tablespoon minced garlic

1 to 3 teaspoons crushed red pepper
1 tablespoon crushed oregano
½ teaspoon salt
3 cups steamed white rice
Salsa (recipe follows)

Mix the oil, vinegar, garlic, pepper, oregano, and salt together and pour the marinade over the meat. Refrigerate for several hours or overnight. Remove the meat from the refrigerator 30 minutes before cooking. Grill the beef quickly, just a minute or two on each side, over hot coals or on a stove-top grill. Serve immediately, with rice and salsa.

Tomato & Green Pepper Salsa

1 large tomato, diced	1 tablespoon red wine
1 green pepper, diced	vinegar
1 tablespoon finely	1 teaspoon chopped
chopped Italian parsley	oregano
2 to 3 tablespoons olive oil	Salt and pepper

Toss all the ingredients together, taste and correct seasonings, and chill until ready to use.

ABOUT MARINADES

Liquid marinades are traditionally made of two primary ingredients—oil and acid—for the purpose of spreading flavor through immersion. A marinade can also provide essential lubrication for grilled foods. Because of its pleasing flavor, olive oil is the customary choice in most marinades, but an extra virgin olive oil is not generally necessary. If a marinated food is to be cooked at high temperatures, a pure olive oil is the best choice. Acids vary depending on the type of food to be marinated and include such diverse items as vinegar, citrus juice, wine, tomatoes or tomato juice, yogurt, buttermilk, and soy sauce. A variety of flavoring agents may be added to influence the taste of the marinade. Garlic, shallots, onions, and herbs are the most common additions, and sugar, mustard, orange flower water, vanilla, ginger, and many other items are commonly added. Occasionally, papaya extract is used for its tenderizing qualities.

I frequently use a favorite vinaigrette as a marinade, especially the redolent Vinaigrette Diane (page 221) and the Black Raspberry Vinaigrette (page 216), both of which are tremendously good with poultry.

Leeks for Mary Frances
Leeks in Mustard Vinaigrette

Serves 4 to 6

I had the joy of preparing lunch in my home for M. F. K. Fisher. At the time, she was working on her book on Dijon, Long Ago in France, *and I wanted the lunch to evoke it in some way. I used a mustard I had brought home from Dijon to prepare a dressing for one of her favorite vegetables.*

12 to 15 young leeks, each no bigger than 1 inch in diameter	**Mustard Vinaigrette, page 215**

Cut off the root ends of the leeks. Cut off most of the green part, leaving just 2 to 4 inches. Beginning at the root end, make a slit up each leek, through most of the white part but leaving the 2 halves connected. Rinse the leeks well under cool water, making sure to remove any dirt or grit that may be lodged in the center. Plunge the leeks into a pot of rapidly boiling water and simmer them until they are tender but not overcooked. Remove the leeks from the pot, refresh them in ice water, and drain them well on paper towels.

Place the leeks in a glass, stainless-steel, or ceramic container and cover them with the vinaigrette. Let the vegetables sit for at least 30 minutes before serving. The leeks are at their best at this point, but will keep for 3 or 4 days in the refrigerator. They should be removed 30 minutes before serving.

Haricots Verts with Vinaigrette

Serves 6 to 8

Haricots verts *are the tiny green beans you see in the markets throughout France. They are tender and delicious, the perfect accompaniment to almost any meal. By themselves, they make a good lunch when there is little time. In many areas of the United States, they are impossible to find, but they are easy to grow yourself. Farm markets often have them, as they are a specialty item grown by smaller farmers.*

1 pound haricots verts or very young Blue Lake green beans
Mustard Vinaigrette (page 215), Walnut Vinaigrette (page 218), or Warm Shallot Vinaigrette (page 223)
Chopped chives and whole chives (if you are using Mustard Vinaigrette)
¼ cup walnut halves, toasted (if you are using Walnut Vinaigrette)
3 strips of bacon or pancetta, cooked and crumbled (if you are using Warm Shallot Vinaigrette)

Drop the beans into a large pot of boiling water and simmer until they are just tender, about 4 or 5 minutes. Drain and refresh in ice water and drain again, well.

Just before serving, heat a small quantity of the vinaigrette in a small skillet, add the beans, toss them, and heat them through. Remove the beans to a serving plate, spoon more dressing over them, and garnish them with the appropriate garnish.

Grilled Onions
with Romesco Sauce

Serves 4 to 6

There's nothing quite like the taste of grilled young torpedo onions, sweet, slightly pungent, tender and crisp at the same time. They are simply wonderful. In flavor and texture, Romesco sauce provides the perfect companion.

2 dozen small torpedo onions, 3 or 4 inches long	**Olive oil** **Romesco Sauce (page 236)**

Remove the root ends and outer skin of the onions and rub each onion with a little olive oil. If the onions are more than 3 or 4 inches long, you may want to blanch them before grilling. Place the onions over hot coals or on a stove-top grill, turning them as they brown.

Either have the sauce prepared in advance or make it while the onions cook. If you decide to make it at the last minute, be sure to soak the peppers in advance.

When the onions are browned on all sides and are slightly soft to the touch, place them on a serving platter. Serve with the *Romesco* sauce on the side.

VARIATION

Serve the onions with Tuna *Tapenade* (page 110) instead of the *Romesco* sauce. Garnish with *Kalamata* olives.

SALADS

Our Garrick's a salad; for in him we see
Oil, vinegar, sugar, and saltness agree!
Oliver Goldsmith, *Retaliation*

Simple Green Salad

Serves 4

It is generally assumed that one puts oil onto salad greens first to protect them from the wilting effect of the harsh vinegar. Not so. Harold McGee dispels that myth in his book The Curious Cook, *revealing that it is oil that is the more quickly absorbed into the cells of the lettuce, causing it to wilt more quickly than it does when dressed with vinegar. Oil does, however, have a much lower surface tension than vinegar and is thus able to coat the leaves. On bare lettuce vinegar simply runs off because its molecules are strongly attracted to one another. By coating the lettuce in oil first and then adding the vinegar, salt, and pepper, you ensure that your salad will be evenly dressed.*

3 tablespoons extra virgin
   olive oil
1 quart very fresh mixed
   salad greens, 1 to 2
   ounces per person

1 tablespoon medium-acid
   (5⅕–6½ percent) red
   wine vinegar
Salt and black pepper to
   taste

Place the olive oil in the bottom of a large salad bowl and add the greens. Gently toss them with your hands until all of the greens are coated with oil. Sprinkle the vinegar over the mixture and toss it again. Add some salt and pepper and serve immediately.

The ideal way to dress a green salad with a more complex vinaigrette is with your hands. Have greens in a large bowl and your hands freshly washed with no lingering traces of soap. Place a few tablespoons of the vinaigrette in the palm of one hand and then rub it with the other hand so that both palms are coated with the dressing. Pick up the leaves of the greens and toss them very gently to transfer the dressing from your hands to the leaves. They should be very lightly coated. Add salt and pepper to the salad and serve immediately. This method is, admittedly, a little messy, and we do not always find ourselves in circumstances that encourage us to plunge quite so literally into our food. The most effective alternative is to place a small quantity of dressing in a large bowl, add the greens, and toss the mixture quickly with your hands.

Simple Tomato Salad

Serves 1 hearty eater and is easily doubled or tripled

This recipe is given in quantities for one person because I usually prepare it just for myself. Eating tomatoes right out of the garden, still warm from the sun, is one of my favorite solitary pastimes. I often prefer just to munch on one as if it were an apple. The recipe yields enough to share with a friend or two as part of a meal and is very easy to double or triple. The most important aspect of this recipe is that it be made with freshly picked, properly grown tomatoes.

3 ripe medium-sized
   tomatoes
3 cloves garlic, sliced
2 tablespoons extra virgin
   olive oil

1 anchovy fillet, mari-
   nated in vinegar (see
   page 118)
2 teaspoons red wine
   vinegar
Salt and pepper

Slice the tomatoes, arrange them on a platter, and top them with the garlic. Drizzle the olive oil over the slices. Chop the anchovy, combine it with the vinegar, and sprinkle the mixture over the tomatoes. Season with salt and pepper and serve.

Sicilian Orange Salad

Serves 4 to 6

Oranges have long been an essential part of the Sicilian diet. This recipe has evolved considerably from the simple combination of oranges, olive oil, salt, and pepper described to me by my friend A. J. His father, Antonio, now in his nineties, enjoys it regularly. The clear, simple tastes in this dish make it an ideal opener for more complex main courses.

6 medium navel oranges
  or blood oranges if
  available
3 to 4 tablespoons best
  quality extra virgin
  olive oil
1 teaspoon champagne
  vinegar

Salt and freshly ground
  black pepper
10 to 12 curls pecorino
  cheese, about 1 inch
  long, made with a
  potato peeler

Using a sharp paring knife, peel the oranges, removing the white, spongy pith completely, and slice them about ¼ inch thick. Arrange the oranges on a serving platter, drizzle them with the olive oil, and sprinkle on the vinegar. Add a little salt and plenty of black pepper. Scatter the curls of *pecorino* over the oranges and serve.

VARIATION
Serve the salad with a mixture of bitter greens; arugula and young, mild *radicchio* make a pleasing combination. Using your hands, toss the greens with the smallest amount of the

olive oil, the vinegar, and a bit of orange juice until they are just lightly coated. Add a little salt and pepper. Place the greens on one half of a serving platter and arrange the oranges on the other half. Scatter the *pecorino* over both and serve.

 # Bread Salad

Serves 4

It is hard to imagine a less pretentious dish than bread salad, known as panzanella *in its native Italy. The possibilities for variations of this rustic meal are nearly endless. The only non-negotiable ingredients are a flavorful vinaigrette and hearty bread to soak it up. I developed this version when I had an abundance of sun-dried tomato bits sitting in my pantry and a lot of left-over* Kalamata *olives, too.*

4 cups 1-inch bread cubes (see Note below)

1 cup Red Wine Vinaigrette (page 214)

2 tablespoons sun-dried tomato bits

Half a small red onion, diced

4 cloves garlic, minced

1 cup Kalamata olives, pitted and diced

1 cup freshly grated pecorino, Parmesan, dry Jack, or Asiago cheese

2 tablespoons Italian parsley, minced

4 tablespoons fresh basil, cut in thin strips

Note: Use day-old Italian, French, or other rustic bread; sourdough is ideal.

Place the bread cubes in a large bowl and toss them with half of the vinaigrette. Let the bread stand for 30 minutes.

Place the sun-dried tomato bits in a small bowl and cover them with the remaining vinaigrette.

Add the red onion, garlic, olives, cheese, parsley, and basil to the bread cubes and toss the mixture together well. If the salad is to be served immediately, add the remaining vinaigrette with the sun-dried tomatoes and toss it again. If it is to be held a while, wait and add the vinaigrette just before serving.

Saucy Melon Salad

Serves 6

A recipe from Madeleine Kamman's fine book, In Madeleine's Kitchen, *inspired this recipe. I was irresistibly drawn to the vanilla in her vinaigrette and developed this salad that captures, I hope, the spirit of the original.*

3 different melons, choosing among cantaloupe, Crenshaw, Honeydew, orange Honeydew, Crane, Canary, or Casaba (consider a variety of colors)

3 tablespoons Southern Comfort liquor

1 large head butter lettuce or red-leaf lettuce

Avocado-Pineapple Vinaigrette, page 220

Salt

Freshly ground black pepper

¼ cup lightly toasted and coarsely chopped macadamia nuts, pecans, or walnuts

6 sprigs fresh mint

Cut the melons in half, scoop out and discard the seeds, and cut half of each melon into wedges about ⅓ inch thick.

Place the wedges in a wide bowl or on a platter. Using the other halves of the melons, make perfectly shaped melon balls and set them aside with the melon wedges. Sprinkle the melon with the Southern Comfort, cover the platter with plastic wrap, and refrigerate the fruit for 30 minutes. Have 6 large salad plates chilling.

Clean the lettuce and arrange several leaves on each of the plates. Add the wedges of melon, arranging them decoratively and alternating the colors. Add the melon balls to each of the plates. Spoon the dressing over each of the salads, and add salt and a few turns of black pepper. Sprinkle the fruit with nuts, add a sprig of mint, and serve immediately.

Pear & Hazelnut Salad

Serves 4

The elements in this pretty salad resonate intriguingly well with one another. The nuttiness of the hazelnut oil and hazelnuts echoes the nutlike flavor of the avocado, and the hint of pear in the vinegar resonates with the fresh fruit itself. A strikingly delicious and harmonious relationship is played out on the palate.

1 head butter lettuce, thin
   outer leaves and core
   removed
1 pear, peeled, cored, and
   cut lengthwise into ⅛-
   inch-thick slices
1 avocado, peeled and cut
   lengthwise into ⅛-inch-
   thick slices

1 cup smoked chicken,
   cut in medium julienne
Hazelnut Vinaigrette,
   page 219
¼ cup hazelnuts, lightly
   toasted and skinned
Borage flowers, if avail-
   able, and several
   strands of chives, for
   garnish

Arrange the butter lettuce on one large platter or 4 serving plates. Divide the pear and avocado slices among the plates or arrange them attractively on the platter. Place the smoked chicken in the center of the salad. Drizzle vinaigrette over the chicken, pears, and avocados. Crush the hazelnuts just slightly and sprinkle them over the salad. Garnish with borage flowers and a few whole strands of chives.

 *Spinach Salad*

Serves 4 to 6

There are probably as many spinach salads in this world as there are cooks, and here I add mine. I make use of blueberry vinegar and fresh blueberries, both of which go very well with spinach, to create a salad that is a little different, while maintaining some of the traditional elements, hard-boiled eggs, onions, and bacon.

2 bunches fresh spinach
3 tablespoons hazelnut oil
1 medium red onion, cut
    into thin rings
3 hard-boiled eggs, cut in
    lengthwise slices, 6 per
    egg, or chopped
    coarsely
¼ pound pancetta
3 tablespoons peanut oil
2 shallots, minced

2 tablespoons blueberry
    vinegar (4.5 percent
    acidity)
¼ teaspoon ground cloves
¼ teaspoon ground all-
    spice
½ teaspoon freshly
    ground black pepper
½ teaspoon salt
1 cup fresh blueberries

Remove the large stems, clean the spinach thoroughly, and dry it on tea towels. Using your hands, coat the leaves very lightly with a bit of the hazelnut oil. Arrange the leaves on a single large platter or on individual serving plates. Place the rings of red onion over the leaves and add the eggs, either arranging the slices or sprinkling the chopped egg over the surface.

Chop the *pancetta* into small dice, and sauté it in 1 ta-

199

blespoon of peanut oil for 4 minutes. Add the shallots and continue to sauté until the shallots are soft. Remove the pan from the heat, add the remaining oil, the blueberry vinegar, and the spices. Taste and correct the seasoning. Pour the dressing over the salad, sprinkle the blueberries over, and serve immediately.

VARIATIONS
Omit the blueberries and use a sherry vinegar instead of a blueberry vinegar.

Or trim, rinse, and dry ½ pound chicken livers. Cut each liver into 4 pieces. Sauté the livers with the *pancetta* and shallots for 2 or 3 minutes on each side, remove them from the pan, and set them aside. Make the salad according to the recipe and arrange the livers over the salad just before adding the warm dressing.

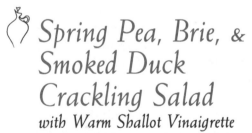

Spring Pea, Brie, & Smoked Duck Crackling Salad
with Warm Shallot Vinaigrette

Serves 4 as a hearty luncheon salad; 8 as a starter

This is a devastating salad, the sort of combination of flavors that makes you want to eat forever, regardless of common sense or consequences. Smoked duck cracklings are delicious by themselves, and the warm vinaigrette makes the Brie melt into everything else, and, Oh, happy day, it's simply divine.

1 quart mesclun or other
young salad greens
Virgin olive oil
Salt and pepper
1 small, 4-inch round of
Brie

1 cup duck cracklings (recipe follows)
1 cup freshly shelled peas,
blanched and freshened
in ice water
Warm Shallot Vinaigrette
(page 223)

Using your hands, very lightly coat the salad greens with olive oil. Sprinkle the greens with salt and pepper, toss them, and arrange them on individual serving plates.

Cut the *Brie* in half vertically. Use a very thin, sharp knife, cut the *Brie* in thin slices and arrange them in circular patterns on top of the greens on each plate. Sprinkle the duck cracklings and peas over the salads, dividing them evenly among the servings. The salad can be held briefly at this point, but no more than 15 minutes.

Just before serving, drizzle each salad with several spoonfuls of the warm vinaigrette and serve immediately.

Smoked Duck Cracklings

Cut the skin of 1 smoked duck into strips measuring ½ inch by 1½ inches. Place the strips in a heavy skillet with ½ cup water over low heat. When the fat has been rendered out of the duck skin, increase the heat to medium. The water will evaporate, and the pieces of skin will be golden and crispy. Remove them with a slotted spoon to a piece of absorbent paper and let them drain. Be sure to keep the temperature of the duck fat below the smoke point. Use a high-range thermometer and keep the temperature between 325°F. and 340°F. Duck cracklings can be made in advance and stored in the refrigerator, but they should be warmed in a 200°F. oven for about 10 minutes before serving.

Warm Vegetable Salad

This hearty salad is perfect in the dark of winter when we crave more robust fare. Served with a simple roasted chicken seasoned only with olive oil, salt, and pepper, it makes a comforting and delicious meal. It is also a welcome addition to a summer barbecue.

2 medium russet (baking)
  potatoes
1 eggplant or 4 Japanese
  eggplants or 4 to 6
  small white eggplants
1 medium-small sweet
  potato
1 medium-small garnet
  yam

4 cups mesclun or mixed
  salad greens, cleaned
  and dry
Red Wine Vinaigrette
  (page 214) or Mustard
  Vinaigrette (page 215)
Edible flowers for garnish

Heat the oven to 425°F. Wash all the vegetables under cool water, scrubbing the potatoes well to remove any clinging dirt or sand. Using the tines of a fork, prick the skins of the root vegetables in several places. Place the baking potatoes directly on the oven rack and let them bake for 1 hour. Reduce the heat to 350°F. If you are using 1 large eggplant, place it in the oven and bake it for 15 minutes. Add the sweet potato and yam to the other vegetables in the oven and bake them for 45 minutes. If you are using the smaller eggplants, place them in the oven for the last 30 minutes. Remove all of the vegetables from the oven and let them rest for 10 minutes.

Place about 2 tablespoons of the vinaigrette in the palms of your hands and rub them together quickly and briefly. Pick up small handfuls of the salad greens, coating them just slightly with the vinaigrette, and arrange them on a large serving platter. Cut each of the potatoes into quarters lengthwise. Cut the eggplants similarly, making more wedges if you are using 1 large eggplant. Arrange the sliced warm vegetables on the bed of greens in a symmetrical, circular pattern. Spoon additional vinaigrette over the vegetables, being sure to cover each slice with a healthy spoonful. Garnish with flowers, if available, and serve immediately.

 *Honeyed Tomato Pasta Salad*

Serves 6 to 8

My daughter Nicolle deserves credit for this recipe. Rummaging through the refrigerator one summer afternoon, she came upon a container of Honey Pepper Vinaigrette and proceeded to create this sweet and summery salad, at its best when cherry tomatoes are freshly picked from the garden.

1 pound small pasta, such as tripolini, small shells, and so on

1 quart ripe cherry tomatoes or 8 or 9 ripe medium-sized tomatoes

8 cloves garlic, minced

4 very small red onions, torpedo if available, thinly sliced

A handful of chopped fresh herbs, such as mint, oregano, and Italian parsley

Honey Pepper Vinaigrette (page 219)

Cook the pasta in plenty of boiling salted water, rinse it, and drain. While the pasta is cooking, cut the cherry tomatoes in half. If you are using larger tomatoes, remove the skins by plunging the tomatoes in boiling water for 10 seconds. The skins will then be easily pulled off. Cut the tomatoes in half crosswise, squeeze them to remove extra juice and seeds, and chop them coarsely. Toss the tomatoes with the garlic, onions, and herbs. Add about ¼ cup of the dressing and toss again. Combine the tomato mixture with the pasta, add the remaining dressing, and toss well. Serve the pasta garnished with sprigs of fresh herbs.

VARIATION

Toss 8 ounces cooked bay shrimp with a little of the dressing and add them to the salad with the rest of the dressing. Toss well.

Sesame Shrimp Pasta Salad
with Corn, Peas, & Cilantro

Serves 8 to 10

This is a sweet and evocative summer salad that shows off its most influential ingredients—toasted sesame oil, rice vinegar, and cilantro—to beautiful advantage. It is a great addition to any summer buffet or barbecue and makes a delightful main course for a brunch or summer luncheon, too.

1 pound small pasta, such as small shells

½ cup corn oil, preferably unrefined

3 tablespoons toasted sesame oil

4 tablespoons unseasoned rice vinegar

Pinch sugar

Salt

1 pound cooked and peeled rock shrimp or bay shrimp

1 cup plus 2 tablespoons Sesame Mayonnaise (page 232)

1 ½ cups fresh corn, cooked on the cob and cut

1 cup fresh peas, blanched

4 tablespoons chopped cilantro leaves

Sprigs of cilantro

Cook the pasta in plenty of boiling, salted water. While the pasta is cooking, mix together both oils, the rice vinegar, and the sugar. Add salt and more vinegar to taste. Drain the pasta, rinse it under cool water, and toss it with just enough of the vinaigrette to coat. Set the pasta mixture aside.

Toss together the shrimp, 1 cup of the sesame mayonnaise, and ¼ cup each of the corn and peas and 1 tablespoon of the chopped cilantro. Taste the mixture, add salt as needed, and set aside. Toss the remaining corn, peas, and vinaigrette with the pasta, along with 2 tablespoons of the chopped cilantro.

Arrange the pasta mixture on a large serving platter and make an indention in the center about 5 inches wide. Fill the center of the pasta with the rock shrimp mixture and crown the salad with the remaining 2 tablespoons sesame mayonnaise. Sprinkle the remaining chopped cilantro leaves over the salad, garnish with sprigs of cilantro, and serve.

 *Wild Rice Salad*

Serves 6 to 8 as an accompaniment; 4 as a main course salad

Once tasted together, wild rice and vanilla seem to plead for each other's company. The perfect vehicle for bringing the two together is balsamic vinegar, which has a whisper of vanilla itself. Much to the delight of my vegetarian friends, this salad is as good without the addition of the smoked poultry.

1 cup (6 ounces) un-
   cooked wild rice
Salt
Vinaigrette Diane (page
   221)
1 shallot, minced

1 cup walnuts, lightly
   toasted
2 tablespoons finely
   minced Italian parsley
1 tablespoon snipped
   chives

1 cup smoked duck or	Sprigs of fresh herbs
smoked chicken meat,	
cut in julienne	

Place the wild rice in a heavy pot with 3 cups of water and a generous pinch of salt. Cook until the rice is tender and the water absorbed, about 40 minutes. Remove the pan from the heat and let the rice rest for 5 minutes. Turn the wild rice out into a large bowl. Add about ¼ cup of the vinaigrette and toss the two together. Coarsely chop the walnuts and add them to the rice, along with the parsley and chives. If you are using it, add all but a few strips of the poultry. Add another ½ cup of the vinaigrette and toss everything together. Place the salad on an attractive serving platter and garnish it with the reserved strips of poultry and sprigs of the fresh herbs. Spoon 2 or 3 more tablespoons of the vinaigrette over the salad just before serving.

 *Cannellini Bean Salad*

Serves 4

Cannellini *beans have a wonderful, creamy texture and get along well with a variety of other ingredients. Great Northern beans or small white navy beans are reliable substitutes, but it is worth the effort to look for the* cannellini. *The canned ones will work in a pinch when you decide, say, on a last-minute picnic. Just be sure to rinse off the juices before you begin the recipe.*

1 cup dried cannellini
beans
2 cups chicken stock
1 small red onion, diced
Several cloves garlic,
minced
2 roasted red peppers, cut
in small julienne

¼ cup chopped Italian
parsley
2 tablespoons chopped
fresh mint
Extra virgin olive oil
Medium-acid (6–6½
percent) red wine
vinegar
Salt and pepper

Cover the beans with water and soak them overnight. Drain the soaking water off and rinse the beans. Place them in a heavy pot with the chicken stock and enough water to cover plus 2 inches. Simmer the beans until they are tender but not falling apart, adding more water if needed. When the beans are done—in approximately 40 minutes—rinse, drain, and cool them.

In a large mixing bowl, toss the cooled beans with the onion, garlic, peppers, parsley, and mint. Add enough olive oil to coat the mixture well. Add vinegar to taste, about ¼ to ⅓ the quantity of oil used. Taste and adjust the quantities of oil and vinegar. Add salt and pepper, toss well, and serve.

VARIATIONS
Serve the bean salad on a bed of fresh salad greens or spinach. Top with a handful of homemade garlic croutons (page 88) and serve with a simple vinaigrette on the side. Garnish with sprigs of Italian parsley.
Or, instead of olive oil, use a blend of ⅓ hazelnut oil and ⅔ peanut oil. Top the salad with ¼ cup lightly toasted hazelnuts.

# Italian Bean Salad

Serves 8 to 10

This is another recipe I developed for my daughter Nicolle. "Include more recipes for beans," she always tells me. They are good for a student's budget and will keep well for several days. Beans also take to a vinaigrette like a fish to water, as they say. This hearty salad is another ideal picnic dish; just be sure to keep it properly chilled.

¾ cup each red beans, small white beans, and black beans
1 cup beef stock
1 each red bell pepper, yellow bell pepper, and orange bell pepper; substitute 1 green bell pepper if all the colors are not available
1 pound Italian sausages
1 small red onion, diced

Several cloves garlic, minced
¼ cup red wine vinegar, medium acid
3 tablespoons chopped Italian parsley
1 teaspoon chopped fresh oregano
½ teaspoon crushed red peppers (optional)
1 cup extra virgin olive oil
Salt and pepper to taste

The night before you plan to serve the salad, place each type of bean in a separate container and cover with water. The next day rinse and drain the beans, and cook them—still separately—until they are tender. Drain, rinse, and let the beans cool. Once the beans have cooled, toss them together with the beef stock and set them aside while you prepare the vegetables.

Remove the stems, seeds, and cores of the peppers and cut them into medium dice. Set aside. Fry or broil the sausages until done. Drain the sausages on absorbent paper and, when they have cooled, cut them into ¼-inch-thick diagonal slices. Add the peppers, sausages, and red onion to the beans and toss everything together.

In a separate bowl, make the vinaigrette by combining the remaining ingredients. Taste the mixture and adjust the seasonings. Pour half of the vinaigrette over the bean salad and toss it well. If the salad is to be served immediately, add as much of the remaining vinaigrette as you like. If the salad is to be held, refrigerate it until 15 minutes before serving and then toss it with the remaining vinaigrette.

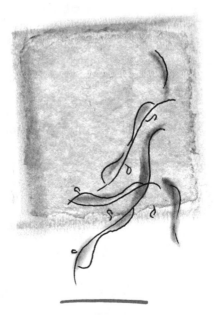

Winter Jewel Salad
with Grilled Lamb Tenderloin

Serves 4

This bright salad sparkles on the palate as well as on the plate. It is beautifully elegant, perfect for a Christmas Eve or New Year's Eve dinner.

1 pomegranate
2 persimmons, ripe but
  slightly firm
1 pound lamb loin
1 quart winter greens,
  such as mesclun or
  arugula

**Cranberry Vinaigrette
  (page 217)**
**Whole cranberries for
  garnish**

Cut the pomegranate in half, remove the seeds, and set it aside. Peel the persimmons, slice them into ¼-inch-thick rounds, and set them aside. Grill or broil the lamb loin until it is medium rare, about 5 or 6 minutes on each side. Let it rest for 5 minutes. While the lamb is resting, toss the greens with just enough cranberry vinaigrette to coat the leaves lightly. Arrange the greens off-center on individual serving plates. Place 2 or 3 slices of persimmon on the greens. Cut the lamb loin into thin slices and arrange them fanned out next to the greens. Spoon a small quantity of the vinaigrette over the persimmons and over the lamb. Sprinkle 2 or 3 tablespoons of pomegranate seeds over each salad, garnish with a few whole cranberries, and serve immediately.

VINAIGRETTES

In earlier times a vinaigrette was a little silver box containing a sponge soaked in vinegar. Used from the late eighteenth century through the late nineteenth century, they were held to a refined nose to eclipse the facts of life and hide them from the upperclass women. The box, with its scent of vinegar, effectively masked the stench of open sewers and exposed garbage.

What is it about the combination of oil and vinegar that makes it so universal, so pervasive and delicious a union? There is no scientific explanation for the pleasure of the taste, but one can draw on one's own experience to understand this union of opposites. The oil provides a soft shield on the tongue from the acetic acid, and the acid adds a bright spark to the tongue-coating richness of the oil. The individual flavors of the two elements add nuance and variation to an already pleasing combination.

Vinaigrettes can be simple or complex, cold or hot, mild or spicy, and used in a broad range of dishes, not just in the salads with which they are most commonly associated. Consider a vinaigrette as a marinade for seafood, poultry, or vegetables to be grilled or as a condiment on sandwiches. Here, I offer my favorites, combinations that, over the years, I have found most pleasing. Some of the recipes, Cranberry Vinaigrette, for instance, call for special ingredients that may not be part of your everyday pantry. As these recipes have been developed with these particular products in mind, substitutes will not be very successful. If an ingredient is unavailable, it is best to choose another recipe.

I encourage you to experiment with your own combinations, using just a few simple guidelines. For a robust, tart vinaigrette, use one part vinegar to three parts oil. For a mellower, smoother mixture, increase the oil to four parts. The flavors in a vinaigrette based on fruit vinegar will be intensified by a pinch of sugar, and in virtually all oil and vinegar mixtures, salt is necessary to blend the flavors properly.

White Wine Vinaigrette

Makes about 1 cup

This is a simple, basic vinaigrette, light but robust, and good wherever a vinaigrette is welcome, on salads of all kinds, including those with light meats such as poultry, pork, or seafood.

3 tablespoons white wine vinegar or champagne vinegar (6–7 percent acidity)
1 tablespoon lemon juice
1 teaspoon dry mustard
1 clove garlic, minced
1 small shallot, minced
3/4 teaspoon salt

1/2 teaspoon freshly ground black pepper
1/4 cup virgin or extra virgin olive oil
1/2 cup pure olive oil
1 tablespoon chopped Italian parsley
1 tablespoon snipped chives

Combine the vinegar, lemon juice, mustard, garlic, shallot, salt, and pepper in a mixing bowl. Whisk in the olive oils until smooth. Add the herbs, taste, and correct the seasoning, adding more salt, pepper, or vinegar as necessary.

Red Wine Vinaigrette

Makes about 1 cup

This is a basic and versatile dressing, suitable whenever a recipe calls for a vinaigrette. Although it will keep refrigerated, it is best when it is first made. As it takes just a few minutes to prepare, make only as much as you will need for a single recipe. If you prefer a milder-tasting vinaigrette, reduce the extra virgin olive oil to ¼ cup and use pure olive oil to complete the recipe.

¼ cup red wine vinegar
  (6–7 percent acidity)
1 teaspoon lemon juice
2 cloves garlic
2 tablespoons minced
  fresh herbs

1 teaspoon Dijon-style
  mustard
¾ teaspoon salt
½ teaspoon freshly
  ground black pepper
¾ cup virgin or extra
  virgin olive oil

Combine the vinegar, lemon juice, garlic, herbs, mustard, salt, and pepper in a mixing bowl. Whisk in the olive oil until smooth. Taste and correct seasoning, adding more salt or pepper as necessary.

Mustard Vinaigrette

Makes 1½ cups

Mustard vinaigrette is excellent with heartier salads and those that contain meat and poultry. I particularly enjoy it with roasted new potatoes and grilled sausages and with Blue Lake green beans. It can be made in advance and will keep refrigerated without any deterioration in flavor for a week. I make mustard vinaigrette with white wine or champagne vinegars, finding that red wine vinegars compete with the mustard for center stage.

2 tablespoons Dijon-style mustard
1 shallot, minced
2 cloves garlic, minced
1 teaspoon finely chopped fresh thyme leaves
1 teaspoon finely chopped Italian parsley

½ teaspoon freshly ground black pepper
½ teaspoon salt
2 tablespoons champagne vinegar
Juice of half a lemon, about 2 tablespoons
½ cup extra virgin olive oil
1 cup pure olive oil

In a medium mixing bowl, whisk together the mustard, shallot, garlic, herbs, salt and pepper, vinegar, and lemon juice. Add the extra virgin olive oil and blend with a whisk until smooth. Add the pure olive oil, whisking to blend the mixture well.

Black Raspberry Vinaigrette

Makes about 2 cups

A low-acid black raspberry vinegar provides the most intense raspberry flavor, one that will hold up in combination with other ingredients. I have heard claims that raspberry vinegar and olive oil do not go well together, but have always found this particular combination to be very successful.

½ cup black raspberry
   vinegar (4.5 percent
   acidity)
2 cloves garlic, minced
¼ teaspoon dry mustard
½ teaspoon sugar

Pinch ground cloves
½ cup extra virgin olive oil
1 cup pure olive oil
¼ teaspoon salt
1 teaspoon fresh, cracked
   black pepper

Combine the vinegar, garlic, mustard, sugar, and cloves in a mixing bowl. Whisk in the extra virgin olive oil until the mixture is smooth, then whisk in the pure olive oil. Add salt and pepper, taste, and correct seasoning, adding more salt, pepper, or sugar as necessary.

Red Raspberry Vinaigrette

Makes about 1 cup

The delicate flavor of red raspberry vinegar goes beautifully with nut oils. Add the chopped walnuts for more walnut flavor and a little texture. This dressing is ideal for any green salad, fruit salad, or salads with chicken or other white meats. Because of the instability of walnut oil, the vinaigrette should be made in small quantities.

¼ cup red raspberry vinegar (4.5 percent acidity)
1 small shallot, minced
¼ teaspoon sugar
2 teaspoons finely minced Italian parsley
1 tablespoon chopped walnuts (optional)

¼ cup walnut oil or hazelnut oil
½ cup refined peanut oil
¼ teaspoon salt
1 teaspoon fresh, cracked black pepper

Combine the vinegar, shallot, sugar, and parsley in a mixing bowl, along with the walnuts, if you are using them. Whisk in the two oils until the mixture is smooth, add salt and pepper, taste, and correct the seasoning, adding more salt, pepper, or sugar as necessary.

Cranberry Vinaigrette

Makes 1⅓ cups

This is a simple yet festive vinaigrette, perfect for dressing a green salad in fall or winter. It is also delicious with turkey or chicken sandwiches.

⅓ cup cranberry vinegar (see Fruit Vinegars, page 145)
1 teaspoon thinly sliced orange peel, all rind removed, cut into ½-inch strips

Pinch ground allspice
Pinch granulated sugar
½ cup hazelnut oil
½ cup refined peanut oil
Pinch salt
¼ teaspoon freshly ground black pepper

Whisk together the vinegar, orange peel, allspice, and sugar. Add the hazelnut oil and whisk until the mixture is smooth. Add the peanut oil, salt, and pepper, whisk, and taste. Add more salt, pepper, or sugar as necessary.

Walnut Vinaigrette

Makes 1¾ cups

Walnut vinaigrette adds a pleasing complexity to a simple green salad. It is also very good with a variety of composed salads, especially those in which poultry or meat and fruit are combined. This dressing is best when used within two or three days of its making, and it should be refrigerated. The recipe can easily be halved.

¼ cup balsamic vinegar
¼ cup Cabernet
   Sauvignon or other
   hearty red wine
1 shallot, minced
2 tablespoons chopped
   walnuts

1 teaspoon freshly ground
   black pepper
⅓ cup walnut oil
1 cup refined peanut oil
Salt to taste

Combine the vinegar, wine, shallot, walnuts, and black pepper in a mixing bowl. Whisk in the walnut oil. Add ⅔ cup of the peanut oil, whisk until the mixture is smooth, and taste the dressing. Add as much of the remaining oil as necessary to reach the proper balance of oil and acid. Add salt to taste.

Hazelnut Vinaigrette

Makes about ¾ cup

Hazelnut oil is delicate and unstable; it becomes rancid quickly. As it is also very expensive, it is best to make this dressing in small quantities. Keep any leftover dressing chilled and use it within a few days.

3 tablespoons pear vine-
   gar (page 145)
1 small shallot, minced
1 teaspoon snipped chives

3 tablespoons hazelnut oil
6 tablespoons peanut oil
Salt and white pepper

In a small mixing bowl, combine the vinegar, shallot, and chives. Whisk in the oils, beginning with the hazelnut oil. Add salt and pepper to taste.

Honey Pepper Vinaigrette

Makes about 1¾ cups

This could also be known as Nicolle's Vinaigrette; she absolutely adores it. Until she discovered it, I used Honey Pepper Vinaigrette only as a dressing for grilled prawns (see page 167). Then she came along and started putting it on green salad, tomatoes, pasta salad, and, well, here it is, waiting for you to discover your own favorite uses for this sweet and spicy combination of flavors. I find it goes deliciously with grilled or broiled lamb.

¼ cup sherry vinegar	1 teaspoon salt
¼ cup wild blackberry honey or other fragrant honey, warmed	1 shallot, minced
	3 cloves garlic, minced
	¼ cup finely chopped mint
2 tablespoons freshly ground black pepper	1 cup olive oil

Combine the vinegar, honey, 1 tablespoon of the pepper, salt, shallot, garlic, and mint. Whisk well and taste. Add the remaining tablespoon of pepper for a stronger pepper taste. Slowly whisk in the olive oil. Use immediately or refrigerate. Remove the dressing from refrigerator 30 minutes before using and whisk it well.

Avocado-Pineapple Vinaigrette

Makes about 1 cup

Originally developed for the Saucy Melon Salad on page 196, this light dressing is outstanding on sliced avocados or seafood salads—especially those of scallops or lobster. It can also be used as a marinade for fish or chicken that is to be grilled.

¼ cup pineapple guava vinegar or pineapple vinegar or 3 tablespoons champagne vinegar plus 1 tablespoon pineapple juice	1 teaspoon pure vanilla extract
	1 tablespoon Southern Comfort liquor (optional)
1 teaspoon honey, warmed	¾ cup avocado oil
2 cloves garlic, mashed	Salt and pepper
	6 to 8 fresh mint leaves, cut in thin strips

Place the vinegar, honey, and garlic in a small bowl, stir to combine well, and let the mixture sit for 20 minutes. Strain the mixture into a larger bowl and discard the garlic. Add the vanilla and Southern Comfort and slowly whisk in the avocado oil. Add salt and pepper to taste, and stir in the mint leaves.

Let the vinaigrette rest, refrigerated, for 20 minutes before using it. If it is chilled longer, let it sit at room temperature for a few minutes and whisk again before using it.

Vinaigrette Diane

Makes about 1 cup

I named this sensational dressing after the writer Diane Ackerman, whose book A Natural History of the Senses *includes the evocative and sensual treatise on vanilla that inspired the recipe. Besides, I kept getting strange looks whenever I mentioned Vanilla Vinaigrette, although the response was terrific if people tasted it without being told what it was. Vanilla is so closely associated with desserts in our minds that the concept seems jarring. It is, however, not jarring to the palate; it is wonderful. I prefer it with poultry, especially smoked duck, and with wild rice. It is also very good with lobster.*

¼ cup balsamic vinegar
1 tablespoon white wine vinegar
1 teaspoon pure vanilla extract
¼ cup walnut oil

½ cup peanut oil
½ teaspoon salt
¼ teaspoon black pepper (about 4 turns of a pepper mill)
¼ teaspoon sugar

Combine the vinegars and vanilla. Whisk in the two oils and add the salt, pepper, and sugar. Taste, adjust seasonings, and refrigerate until you are ready to use it.

Thai Vinaigrette

Makes about 1 cup

Thai vinaigrette is excellent with salads made with grilled meats, especially quail, duck, and beef. Toss some mint leaves and cilantro leaves with other salad greens, top with slices of grilled meat or poultry, and finish with Thai Vinaigrette.

2 cloves garlic, peeled

2 Thai chili peppers or 1 serrano chili pepper

1 tablespoon each minced cilantro leaves, mint leaves, and Thai basil leaves

3 tablespoons fresh lime juice

2 tablespoons rice vinegar

4 teaspoons Thai fish sauce (nam pla)

2 teaspoons sugar

½-inch piece fresh ginger, peeled and chopped

1 cup unrefined peanut oil

In a mortar and pestle pound together the garlic, chili peppers, and herbs or purée them in a blender or food processor. Place the mixture in a small bowl and add the lime juice, vinegar, fish sauce, and sugar. Place the chopped ginger in a garlic press and press the juice into the mixture. Mix the ingredients together and slowly whisk in the oil.

Warm Shallot Vinaigrette

This vinaigrette is best prepared just before serving. Have all your ingredients ready to go; the actual cooking time is very short. Shallot Vinaigrette is delicious on most types of cooked vegetables, especially asparagus, green beans, Brussels sprouts, and fresh artichoke hearts. It is also delicious with a warm seafood salad.

3 tablespoons clarified
butter
4 shallots, finely minced
2 cloves garlic, finely
minced
3 to 4 tablespoons
medium- to high-acid
white wine vinegar

2 tablespoons finely
minced Italian parsley
½ cup oil, such as virgin
olive oil, canola, avo-
cado, or peanut oil

Heat the clarified butter in a small, heavy skillet. Sauté the shallots until they are soft, add the garlic, and sauté for another 2 minutes. Add the vinegar and Italian parsley, sauté for 2 minutes, add the oil, and remove from the heat.

Warm Tomato Vinaigrette

Makes approximately 3 cups

Warm Tomato Vinaigrette is a quick and delicious way of using garden tomatoes at the peak of their season. Serve it over pasta, rice, seafood, poached chicken breasts, and quickly steamed zucchini. Its flavor improves for a couple of days after it is made and it is good chilled, too. Warm, it makes a wonderful dip for fresh vegetables and cheese tortellini *on skewers.*

1 pound in-season, ripe
   tomatoes
½ cup extra virgin olive oil
2 or 3 shallots minced
3 or 4 cloves garlic,
   minced
3 to 4 tablespoons white
   wine vinegar (up to 6½
   percent acidity)

Juice of half a lemon
2 tablespoons fresh herbs,
   such as fresh basil, oregano, chives, Italian parsley, marjoram, and
   thyme
Salt and fresh, cracked
   black pepper

Peel the tomatoes by plunging them into boiling water for 10 seconds. Remove, plunge them into ice water, drain, and remove the skins, which should come off easily. Core the tomatoes, cut them in half, discard the seeds, and chop them coarsely. Heat 2 to 3 tablespoons of the olive oil in a heavy pan and sauté the shallots until they are soft. Add the garlic, sauté for another 2 minutes, add the tomatoes, and stir until they are heated through. Add the remaining olive oil, the vinegar, lemon juice, and fresh herbs, and toss the ingredients together lightly. Remove from the heat, add salt and pepper, and taste. Adjust the seasoning and acidity, adding more vinegar or lemon juice for a tarter sauce.

VARIATIONS

After peeling the tomatoes, cut them into quarters. Sauté the tomatoes first, about 1½ minutes on each side. Remove them from the pan to a warmed serving bowl. Sauté 1 minced *jalapeño* chili pepper along with the shallots. Toss all the ingredients together and use cilantro in place of the mixed herbs.

Or add 3 tablespoons *Kalamata* olives, pitted and coarsely chopped, to the mixture along with the lemon juice, vinegar, and oil.

SAUCES

Cherry & Corn Salsa

Makes about 3 to 4 cups

There is only a short period in early summer when you can make this delicate summer salsa. In June, the first of summer's corn coincides with cherry season. Because salmon is also plentiful at that time, I recommend your serving this salsa with freshly grilled or poached wild salmon. It is also an excellent accompaniment to gravlax or fresh smoked salmon.

1 pound ripe cherries, such as Bing or Ranier, or a combination

2 ears of fresh white corn, shucked

2 medium shallots, minced

1 small jalapeño chili pepper, seeds and stem removed; minced

2 teaspoons minced fresh spearmint or peppermint

1 teaspoon minced fresh thyme

3 tablespoons unrefined corn oil

2 tablespoons medium-acid vinegar, such as cherry, raspberry, or sherry

¼ teaspoon salt

Remove the pits from the cherries, cut them into quarters, place them in a mixing bowl, and set them aside. Place the corn in a large pot of cold water and place the pot over high heat. When the water comes to a boil, remove the corn and plunge it immediately into cold water. Drain on paper towels, cut the kernels from the cobs, and add them to the bowl of cherries. Add the remaining ingredients and toss well. Taste the salsa and correct the seasoning, adding more vinegar if it is overly sweet and a pinch more salt if necessary. Let the salsa rest for 30 minutes before serving it.

# Mango Salsa

Makes about 3 cups

Use this salsa on grilled chicken, grilled seafood, or chilled smoked salmon. It is also an excellent accompaniment to curries. Because of the delicacy of the flavors in this salsa, it is the perfect place to use one of the lighter extra virgin olive oils from the south of France or from Italy's Liguria region, such as the delicate late-harvest biancardo made by Ardoino.

2 ripe mangos (not too soft)
1 medium red onion
1 jalapeño or serrano chili pepper
¼ cup cilantro leaves

Juice of 1 lime
3 to 4 tablespoons rice vinegar
3 tablespoons mild extra virgin olive oil
Salt

Peel the mango with a sharp knife and cut the flesh off the seed in thick pieces as best you can. Cut the slices into ¼-

inch cubes and be sure to cut off and use any flesh that has clung to the seed, as well. Place the cubed mango in a medium bowl.

Cut the onion into ¼-inch dice and add it to the mango. Remove the seed and stem from the pepper, mince it finely, and add it to the mango, along with the cilantro leaves, lime juice, vinegar, and oil. Toss the ingredients together, add just a pinch of salt, toss again, and taste. Correct the seasonings by adding more lime juice, vinegar, and salt as necessary.

CLASSIC MAYONNAISE

Mayonnaise is the classic cold emulsion, an oil-in-water mixture, the oil suspended in the raw egg yolks with the help of a small quantity of lemon juice and vinegar. It is the essential building block for a panorama of classic and new, modest and sophisticated, sauces that crown everything from hamburgers to lobster salads. As we all know, it is the easiest thing in the world to grab a jar of commercial mayonnaise off the shelf, but not even the best available will provide the taste, texture, or satisfaction of mayonnaise prepared in one's own kitchen.

Oil is by quantity the primary ingredient in this classic emulsion and should be carefully chosen. Because I enjoy the taste of a strong, green olive oil, that is what I use when I make mayonnaise for my own use. It is, however, a very personal matter, and many people consider mayonnaise made with pure olive oil unpleasantly strong; they will recommend your cutting it at least by half with corn oil. Choose an oil to suit your palate, and one that is fresh or has been properly stored so that there is no trace of rancidity. If it is important to you, you should also consider making the healthiest choice possible and use an oil high in monounsaturated fatty acids, the type considered most beneficial to our health. Olive oil has the highest percentage, and is the most readily available and best tasting of your choices. If its intense flavor is objectionable to you, choose one of the milder-tasting oils available—canola or avocado, for example.

The same care must be taken with the acids in the sauce; everyone senses levels of acidity differently. If you prefer intense tartness, use a higher-acid vinegar and more lemon juice. I prefer a rich, full-bodied vinegar with a lower acid level, up to 6 percent, and prefer the vinegar flavor to be mellowed with a healthy dose of citrus.

The true, classic mayonnaise does not contain mustard, but recipes do include the instructions to "bind" the sauce with the addition of boiling water as the final step in preparation. My experimenting in the kitchen has never proven this to be necessary, and my experience is backed up by Harold McGee, who writes on the science of food, and tells us that the only reason to add water is to adjust the consistency of an overly stiff mayonnaise.

When discussing cold emulsions that are made with egg yolks, it has become necessary to address questions of health and safety. In the northeastern part of the United States, there have been problems with *salmonella* in both eggs and chickens, problems born of crowded conditions, poor sanitation, and the resulting contamination of the crowded chicken coops. The scare shot like wildfire through the nation, and I have heard many food professionals claim that the use of raw eggs now belongs to history. The statistics bear out that the problem has been both limited and regional. You must, however, decide this issue for yourself. What chances are you going to take? If you are concerned, I recommend your checking with your local health department for information about outbreaks of *salmonella* in your area. If you live in a rural area, or have easy access to a farm community, I encourage you to find a reliable egg farmer and get your eggs fresh from the source. I do not recommend that you give up raw eggs, certainly not without a serious fight. Surely, with all of the recent advances in sanitation and technology, we can find a way to continue to use what has been a culinary staple for centuries—something safer and more environmentally sensitive than the irradiation of food that is currently being suggested.

Properly refrigerated, homemade mayonnaises and their cousins will easily keep at least a week to ten days, although they are so good I have never had them stick around that long.

Handmade Mayonnaise

Makes 1½ cups

3 egg yolks, at room
  temperature
¼ teaspoon salt
¼ teaspoon ground white
  pepper
¼ cup extra virgin olive oil
1 cup corn oil

2 teaspoons medium-acid
  champagne vinegar
1 to 2 tablespoons lemon
  juice
1 tablespoon water
  (optional)

With a whisk combine the egg yolks, salt, and pepper. Add the oil a teaspoon at a time, stirring vigorously after each addition. As the sauce thickens, you may add progressively more oil and, finally, the vinegar and lemon juice. If necessary, add water to achieve the desired consistency. Refrigerate for 2 hours before using.

Mayonnaise Made in the Blender

Makes 1½ cups

The trouble with emulsions made in the blender is that the air incorporated into them acts as a cushion on the tongue, dulling the taste somewhat. It is often necessary to increase the flavoring agents, so you should taste the emulsion frequently until you find the proportions that suit your palate.

1 whole egg, at room temperature

1 egg yolk, at room temperature

2 to 3 teaspoons vinegar

½ teaspoon salt

¼ teaspoon ground white pepper

1 teaspoon prepared mustard

1¼ cups oil

1 to 2 tablespoons lemon juice

1 tablespoon boiling water, if needed

Place the whole egg, egg yolk, vinegar, salt, pepper, and mustard into your blender or food processor and process for 30 seconds. Slowly add the oil in a steady stream, continuing to process the entire time. Add the lemon juice to taste.

If the sauce has become particularly stiff, add the boiling water to achieve the proper consistency. Place the mayonnaise in a nonreactive container and let it rest in the refrigerator for at least 2 hours before using it.

Flavored Mayonnaises

Using either of these basic recipes as a framework, you can create a kaleidoscope of flavored mayonnaises by changing the vinegar and oil you use, by eliminating the lemon juice, or by varying the type of mustard. Classic mayonnaise serves as the basis for more complex sauces, such as Rémoulade Sauce, Tartare Sauce, and the well-known if not revered Thousand Island Dressing. Mastering the classic version and sculpting it to your preference will greatly increase your culinary versatility. If you make a flavored vinegar of which you are particularly fond, see how it works in a mayonnaise. For fruit-flavored mayonnaises, you will need to add 1 or 2 teaspoons of sugar to draw out the full flavor of the fruit. Where I have omitted the lemon juice, increase the quantity of other acids to reach the proper taste and consistency. Unless otherwise specified, I recommend low-to medium-acid vinegars, no higher than 60 grain (6 percent). These are my favorite combinations. (For the various vinegars, see Flavored Vinegars, pages 144–153.)

CRANBERRY Use cranberry vinegar and omit the lemon juice.
CRANBERRY-ORANGE Use cranberry vinegar, substitute orange juice for the lemon juice, and use ¼ cup walnut oil and 1 cup peanut oil.

POMEGRANATE Use homemade pomegranate vinegar and omit the lemon juice.

BLUEBERRY Use a low-acid (4.5–5 percent) blueberry vinegar, omit the lemon juice, and add a healthy pinch of ground allspice or cloves.

RASPBERRY-WALNUT Use a low- to medium-acid (up to 6 percent) red raspberry vinegar, omit the lemon juice, and use ¼ cup walnut oil and 1 cup peanut oil.

BLACK RASPBERRY Use a low-acid (4.5–5 percent) black raspberry vinegar, omit the lemon juice, and add 2 cloves garlic, raspberry mustard (omit if unavailable), and 1 teaspoon sugar.

SESAME Use rice vinegar, omit the lemon juice, and use ¼ cup toasted sesame oil, 1 cup peanut or corn oil, and 1 teaspoon sugar.

ROSEMARY Use 1 to 2 tablespoons red wine vinegar infused with fresh rosemary and garlic, cut the lemon juice to 1 teaspoon, and add ½ teaspoon very finely minced fresh rosemary.

HERB To the eggs in the blender, add 2 cloves garlic and use champagne vinegar. After completing the mayonnaise, stir in by hand 3 tablespoons finely chopped fresh herbs, such as Italian parsley, oregano, thyme, lemon thyme, tarragon, basil, and marjoram.

CUCUMBER AND DILL Use homemade cucumber vinegar, 1 teaspoon fresh dill, and ⅛ teaspoon dill seed.

CHIPOTLE PEPPER Omit the vinegar and white pepper, add 1 to 2 tablespoons of canned *chipotle* peppers puréed with their sauce, and substitute lime juice for the lemon juice. If available, use unrefined corn oil. When the sauce is finished, stir in by hand 2 tablespoons finely chopped cilantro.

VANILLA Omit the mustard and lemon juice, use vanilla oil

(page 86) and rice vinegar, balsamic vinegar, or sherry vinegar, and add 1 teaspoon sugar.

AÏOLIS & THEIR COUSINS

Aïoli is the peasant cousin of mayonnaise, robust where mayonnaise is subtle, wild where mayonnaise is tame. Some variations are full of fire where the mellow mother sauce is mild, soothing, and, it might be said, bland. It is a short leap from homemade mayonnaise to this family of velvety garlic sauces known as skordalia, *rouille, romesco, allioli,* and, most famously, *aïoli.* Throughout the Mediterranean region, versions of this paste of olive oil and garlic have been used to garnish fish stews. The specific ingredients vary with the region, but the basic concept and the technique for producing it have much in common.

Traditionally, garlic was ground into a paste with a small quantity of salt and some egg yolks in a mortar with a pestle. Olive oil was slowly added to form a thick, rich emulsion. Potatoes, breadcrumbs, tomatoes, peppers—hot and sweet, ground and fresh—vinegar, lemon juice, and almonds all make appearances in the regional panorama of sauces, depending on the local flair. *Aïoli* itself comes to us from Provence in southeastern France, where its pervasive use has earned it the name, the Butter of Provence. Huge summer feasts held in villages throughout Provence feature *Aïoli monstre,* an enormous buffet of meats, snails, chicken, eggs, and raw and cooked vegetables, all accompanied by grand bowls of *aïoli* and robust red wine.

Many purists claim that the traditional method produces the best aïoli, but it is difficult these days to indulge in the luxury of the slow grinding of garlic by hand. A perfectly delicious *aïoli*—as well as most of its exotic cousins—can be made quickly in a food processor. Remember, it is better to make *aïoli* in a processor than to not make *aïoli* at all. Serve *aïoli* with fresh vegetables, as a sauce for any type of seafood or meat, as a topping for soups and stews, and in place of mayonnaise in sandwiches. It is best to let a fresh *aïoli* rest for at least two hours before serving it.

Several of these sauces call for lemon juice instead of vinegar, but I have included them in this section because they clearly demonstrate one of the most sublime marriages of oil and acid and, frequently enough, they call for vinegar.

The intensity of garlic varies greatly throughout the year. Freshly harvested spring garlic, particularly the pink garlic from Mexico, can be particularly fiery. The last of the garlic, used while we are waiting for the new harvest, can be very mild and bland. Adjust the quantity accordingly.

Aïoli, by Hand

Makes 1¾ to 2 cups

6 to 8 cloves garlic (see sidebar above)
1 teaspoon salt
3 egg yolks, at room temperature

1½ to 2 cups best-quality extra virgin olive oil
2 tablespoons lemon juice

Peel the garlic and, using a pestle, pound it with the salt in a mortar until it becomes a smooth paste. If your mortar is small, transfer the mixture to a larger bowl and whisk in the egg yolks. Add the oil a few drops at a time, whisking until each addition is well incorporated into the mixture before adding more. Gradually increase the quantity of oil with each addition, but never add more oil than is completely absorbed by the mixture.

After you have added half the olive oil, alternate additions of the remaining oil with small quantities of the lemon juice. The final mixture should be the texture of a firm mayonnaise. Taste the *aïoli* and add more lemon juice or more salt to taste.

Aïoli, by Machine

Makes about 1¾ cups

1 whole egg, at room
  temperature
2 egg yolks, at room
  temperature
1 teaspoon Dijon-style
  mustard or 1 teaspoon
  powdered mustard

4 to 10 fresh cloves of garlic, peeled (see sidebar
  on page 234)
½ teaspoon salt
¾ cup extra virgin olive oil
¾ cup olive oil
2 tablespoons lemon juice
  and more to taste
Pinch cayenne pepper

Place the egg, egg yolks, mustard, garlic, and salt in a food processor. Process until the mixture is pulverized. With the machine running, slowly drizzle in the extra virgin olive oil. Add the lemon juice. With the machine still running, drizzle in the olive oil. Taste the mixture, add the cayenne, and more salt or lemon juice to taste.

Romesco Sauce

Makes about 2 cups

Romesco sauce has its roots in the Catalan region of Spain where almond trees flourish along with the olive trees. It is delicious on seafood stew, its traditional use, but is also wonderful with grilled vegetables and as a spicy dip for prawns and scallops.

2 small dried red chili
   peppers
2 egg yolks, at room
   temperature
5 cloves garlic
¼ cup toasted, slivered
   almonds
1 sweet red bell pepper,
   roasted, peeled, and
   seeded

1 small tomato, peeled
   and seeded
1¼ cup extra virgin olive
   oil
¼ cup medium- to high-
   acid (up to 7.5 percent)
   red wine vinegar
Juice of 1 lemon

At least 2 hours before making the sauce, cover the dried peppers with hot water and set them aside.

Drain the dried peppers and place them in a food processor along with egg yolks, garlic, and almonds and process until ingredients are a smooth paste. Add the sweet pepper and tomato. With the machine still running, slowly add half of the olive oil. Stop the processor as necessary to push ingredients down from the sides of the container. Continuing to process, slowly add the vinegar and the lemon juice, followed by the remainder of the olive oil. The sauce will keep for several weeks, but store it in the refrigerator until you are ready to use it.

Skordalia

Makes about 1 cup

This hearty, fiery sauce originated in Greece and is made of garlic pounded to a paste and combined with potatoes. Traditionally, skorthaliá uses almonds instead of potatoes, and the following version was developed because almonds became, and remain, very expensive. It is generally served as an accompaniment to grilled and fried vegetables, chicken, or fish but, for a startlingly delicious dish, substitute this rich mixture for the traditional bland mashed potatoes that seal Shepherd's Pie, a British dish of ground beef, gravy, and onions. The substitute will surely raise a British eyebrow or two, but delight the more adventurous palate. I like the mixture served simply, on mild crackers or thin slices of good French bread.

This version must be made by hand with a mortar and pestle or in a bowl because a food processor will ruin the texture of the potatoes.

½ pound russet (baking)
   potatoes
3 or 4 cloves garlic
1 teaspoon salt
1 egg yolk, at room
   temperature

½ cup extra virgin olive oil
1 tablespoon lemon juice
   or 1 tablespoon hearty
   red wine vinegar, more
   to taste

Bake the potatoes at 350°F. until they are tender, about 45 minutes. Let them cool for 15 minutes, peel them, and press them through a potato ricer or mash them with a fork until they are smooth and fluffy.

Pound the garlic and salt in a mortar with a pestle until the mixture is fairly smooth. Add the egg yolk to the garlic and blend it in well. Add the garlic mixture to the potatoes and, with a wooden spoon, beat the ingredients together until they form a smooth paste. Add the oil, about 3 tablespoons at a time, beating well after each addition. After the oil has been incorporated, add the lemon juice or vinegar. Taste the mixture and correct the seasoning if necessary. The skordalia will be fairly dense but light, with a strong garlic taste, making it a perfect accompaniment for hearty stews and soups.

 Rouille

Makes approximately 1½ cups

This smoldering garlic sauce will wake up the sleepiest, most jaded palate in record time. I have come across several versions of this Mediterranean sauce, some that use bell pepper and a mere two cloves of garlic, some that call for pimientos instead of hot peppers. The timid palate may not concur, but when it comes to pepper and garlic, I say, why hold back? This version, adapted from the inimitable Book of Garlic *by Lloyd J. Harris, does not know the meaning of the word restraint. Serve it with seafood stews, potato soups, or simply a good bread.*

¼ cup red wine vinegar
   (6 percent acidity)
½ cup, packed, fresh
   breadcrumbs
10 cloves garlic, peeled
   and coarsely chopped

1 teaspoon salt
2 teaspoons dried hot red
   pepper flakes
½ cup extra virgin olive oil

Pour the vinegar over the breadcrumbs and let the mixture sit for 30 minutes. Squeeze out the vinegar and discard it. Place the garlic in a large mortar or bowl, along with the salt. Pound slowly, until the garlic has become a fine paste. Add the red pepper flakes and breadcrumbs and pound until they are well incorporated. Add the oil a tablespoon at a time, pounding slowly and steadily after each addition until the oil has been completely incorporated. The finished sauce should be a smooth paste that will keep its shape on a spoon. Refrigerate until you are ready to use it.

PART FIVE

Appendix

GLOSSARY OF TERMS

For descriptions of specific ingredients, see the Glossary of Oils and Vinegars, pages 75–81.

ACETIC ACID A colorless, organic acid (CH_3COOH) produced in fermented liquids by acetobacters

ACETOBACTER The classification of a group of bacteria that digest alcohol and produce acetic acid in the process

ACIDITY The state or degree of the presence of acetic acid

AROMA A characteristic and pleasant odor

BATTERIA Italian name for a series of twelve wooden casks in diminishing sizes used to age *aceto balsamico tradizionale*

CHOLESTEROL A chemical constituent ($C_{27}H_{45}OH$) of all animals and animal tissue

COLD-PRESSED The process by which the juice of the olive (the oil) is extracted mechanically, without recourse to heat or chemicals

DEMIJOHN A large glass or earthenware bottle with a narrow neck; frequently encased in wicker

ESTERS Aromatic molecules produced by the interaction of alcohol and acids and contributing subtle elements of flavor to wine and vinegar

EXPELLER-PRESSED A mechanical process by which oil is extracted from raw material; no chemicals are used in the process, but the seed, nut, or grain may be heated before extraction

FATTY ACID A large group of acids forming the major building blocks of fats in plant, animal, and human cells; major component of membranes surrounding cells; the most common include palmitic, linoleic, stearic, and oleic

FERMENTATION A group of chemical reactions that convert organic compounds into simple substances, as in yeast's anaerobic conversion of sugar into alcohol and carbon dioxide

FIRST PRESS The initial, mechanical pressing, generally of olives, that releases the best of the fruit's juices

HDL High-density lipoprotein, considered the beneficial form of cholesterol

HORIZONTAL DECANTER A modern, continuous method of extracting oil from olives

LDL Low-density lipoprotein, considered the harmful form of cholesterol

MONOUNSATURATED FATTY ACID A fatty acid with only one double carbon bond

MOTHER The gelatinous mat of bacteria that forms across the top of a liquid as acetobacters convert it to vinegar

MUST The cooked juice of grapes before fermentation has begun

OLEIC ACID A highly fluid, monounsaturated fatty acid found in olive, almond, and other seed oils and the membranes of the cells of most plants and animals, including humans

ORLEANS PROCESS The slow method of vinegar production by which the substrate, inoculated with acetobacters, is placed in small tanks or barrels so that only a small surface area is exposed to oxygen

OXIDIZE To combine with oxygen, a process that speeds the spoilage and discoloration of foods, including oils

POLYUNSATURATED FATTY ACID A fatty acid with two or more double carbon bonds

RANCIDITY Decomposition of an oil, generally through excessive exposure to heat, light, or oxygen, and resulting in a harsh, unpleasant taste and smell; unrefined oils are susceptible to rancidity and should be stored in a cool, dry, dark place and used within a reasonable time

SATURATED FATTY ACID A fatty acid the molecules of which are completely filled with hydrogen bonds

SUBSTRATE The original liquid—wine, apple cider, beer, for example—upon which acetobacters feed to produce acetic acid and, thereby, vinegar

VISCOSITY Informally, refers to the degree of oiliness or thickness of an oil; technically, refers, in a liquid, to the degree of resistance to flow

TASTING NOTES

Extra Virgin Olive Oils

Source Country _____ Brand Name _____
Place of Purchase _____ Cost _____
Color/Appearance _____ Aroma _____
Consistency _____ Taste _____ Finish _____
Notes _____
_____

Overall Opinion _____ Will purchase again _____

Source Country _____ Brand Name _____
Place of Purchase _____ Cost _____
Color/Appearance _____ Aroma _____
Consistency _____ Taste _____ Finish _____
Notes _____
_____

Overall Opinion _____ Will purchase again _____

Source Country _____ Brand Name _____
Place of Purchase _____ Cost _____
Color/Appearance _____ Aroma _____
Consistency _____ Taste _____ Finish _____
Notes _____
_____

Overall Opinion _____ Will purchase again _____

TASTING NOTES

Pure Olive Oil

Source Country _____ Brand Name _____

Place of Purchase _____ Cost _____

Color/Appearance _____ Aroma _____

Consistency _____ Taste _____ Finish _____

Notes _____

_____

Overall Opinion _____ Will purchase again _____

Source Country _____ Brand Name _____

Place of Purchase _____ Cost _____

Color/Appearance _____ Aroma _____

Consistency _____ Taste _____ Finish _____

Notes _____

_____

Overall Opinion _____ Will purchase again _____

Source Country _____ Brand Name _____

Place of Purchase _____ Cost _____

Color/Appearance _____ Aroma _____

Consistency _____ Taste _____ Finish _____

Notes _____

_____

Overall Opinion _____ Will purchase again _____

TASTING NOTES

Other Oils

Nut • Vegetable Seed • Flavored

Type of Oil _____ Place of Purchase _____

Brand _____ Cost _____ Refined/Unrefined _____

Taste of raw product _____ Aroma _____

Notes _____

_____

Overall Opinion _____ Will purchase again _____

Type of Oil _____ Place of Purchase _____

Brand _____ Cost _____ Refined/Unrefined _____

Taste of raw product _____ Aroma _____

Notes _____

_____

Overall Opinion _____ Will purchase again _____

Type of Oil _____ Place of Purchase _____

Brand _____ Cost _____ Refined/Unrefined _____

Taste of raw product _____ Aroma _____

Notes _____

_____

Overall Opinion _____ Will purchase again _____

TASTING NOTES

Vinegars

Red Wine • White Wine • Champagne • Sherry • Raspberry • Fruit •
Herb • Balsamic • Malt • Cider • Black • Pineapple

Type of Vinegar _____ Place of Purchase _____

Brand _____ Cost _____ Acidity (Grain) _____

Color _____ Clarity _____ Aroma/Bouquet _____

Body _____ Taste _____

Notes _____

_____

Overall Opinion _____ Will purchase again _____

Type of Vinegar _____ Place of Purchase _____

Brand _____ Cost _____ Acidity (Grain) _____

Color _____ Clarity _____ Aroma/Bouquet _____

Body _____ Taste _____

Notes _____

_____

Overall Opinion _____ Will purchase again _____

Type of Vinegar _____ Place of Purchase _____

Brand _____ Cost _____ Acidity (Grain) _____

Color _____ Clarity _____ Aroma/Bouquet _____

Body _____ Taste _____

Notes __ _____

_____

Overall Opinion _____ Will purchase again _____

BIBLIOGRAPHY

Ackerman, Diane. *A Natural History of the Senses.* New York: Random House, 1990.

Anderson, Burton. "The Balmy Realm of Aceto Balsamico." *Journal of Gastronomy* 4 no. 4 (Winter 1988–1989).

Andrews, Glenn. *Making Flavored Oils & Vinegars.* Pownal, Vt.: Garden Way Publishing, 1989.

Bittman, Mark. "Vinegar Vignettes." *The Gourmet Retailer,* February 1991.

Brooks, Jeffree Sapp. *The Art of Accompaniment.* San Francisco: North Point Press, 1988.

"Can Olive Oil Help the Heart?" *Consumer Reports,* October 1991.

Composition of Foods. Agricultural Handbook no. 8, USDA, 1963.

Cruess, W. V., and M. A. Joslyn. "Home and Farm Preparation of Vinegar." United States Department of Agriculture, circular no. 332, January 1934.

de Groot, Roy Andries. *The Auberge of the Flowering Hearth.* New York: Ballantine, 1973.

Diggs, L. J. *Vinegar.* San Francisco: Quiet Storm Trading Company, 1989.

Dolamore, Anne. *The Essential Olive Oil Companion.* Topsfield, Mass.: Salem House Publishers, 1989.

Dolnick, Edward. "The Mystery of the Healthy French Heart." *In Health,* May/June 1990.

Erasmus, Udo. *Fats and Oils.* Vancouver: Alive Books, 1986.

Field, Carol. *Celebrating Italy*. New York: William Morrow, 1991.

Foods & Nutrition Encyclopedia, 1st ed. Vols. 1 & 2. Clovis, Calif.: Pegus Press, 1983.

Goldstein, Joyce. *The Mediterranean Kitchen*. New York: William Morrow, 1989.

Gunstone, F. D., et al., eds. *The Lipid Handbook*. Vol. 4. London: Chapman and Hall, 1986.

Harris, Lloyd J. *The Book of Garlic*. Reading, Mass.: Aris Books/Addison-Wesley, 1974.

Johnson, Marsha Peters. *Gourmet Vinegars*. Lake Oswego, Oreg.: n.d.

Kamman, Madeleine. *The Making of a Cook*. New York: Atheneum, 1971.

―――. *In Madeleine's Kitchen*. New York: Atheneum, 1984.

Kapp, Cornelia. "Time in a Bottle." *Food Arts*, November 1990.

Karoff, Barbara. *South American Cooking*. Reading, Mass.: Aris Books/Addison-Wesley, 1989.

Klein, Maggie Blyth. *The Feast of the Olive*. Reading, Mass.: Aris Books/Addison-Wesley, 1983.

Lake, Mark, and Judy Ridgway. *Oils, Vinegars, & Seasonings*. New York: Simon and Schuster, 1989.

Madison, Deborah. *The Greens Cook Book*. New York: Bantam Books, 1987.

―――. *The Savory Way*. New York: Bantam Books, 1990.

McGee, Harold. *On Food and Cooking*. New York: Charles Scribner's Sons, 1984.

―――. *The Curious Cook*. San Francisco: North Point Press, 1990.

"Olive Oil." *Consumer Reports,* October 1991.

Ornstein, Robert, Ph.D., and David Sobel, M.D. *Healthy Pleasures.* Reading, Mass.: Addison-Wesley, 1989.

Pastorio, Bob. "Sweet and Sour." *USAir Magazine,* January 1991.

Pellegrini, Angelo. *The Unprejudiced Palate.* San Francisco: North Point Press, 1984.

Plagemann, Catherine, and M. F. K. Fisher. *Fine Preserving.* Reading, Mass.: Aris Books/Addison-Wesley, 1986.

"Quick and Easy Gift Idea: Flavored Vinegars." *Sunset Magazine,* December 1990.

Rombauer, Irma, and Marion Rombauer Becker. *The Joy of Cooking.* New York: Bobbs-Merrill, 1976.

Root, Waverly. *The Food of Italy.* New York: Vintage Books, 1977.

———. *Food.* New York: Simon and Schuster, 1980.

Schlesinger, Sarah, and Barbara Earnest. *The Low Cholesterol Olive Oil Cookbook.* New York: Villard, 1990.

Simeti, Mary Taylor. *Pomp and Sustenance.* New York: Alfred A. Knopf, 1989.

Stapleton, Michael. *The Illustrated Dictionary of Greek and Roman Mythology.* New York: Peter Bedrick Books, 1978.

Stoner, Carol Hupping. *Stocking Up.* Emmaus, Penn.: Rodale Press, 1977.

Swern, Daniel, ed. *Bailey's Industrial Oil and Fat Products,* 4th ed. Vols. 1 & 2. New York: John Wiley and Sons, 1979.

Wolfert, Paula. *The Cooking of South-West France.* New York: Dial Press, 1983.

RESOURCES

This list is not meant to be comprehensive; there are numerous mail order facilities and trade organizations throughout the country. Instead, this brief listing offers the best resources available to anyone having difficulty finding products mentioned in this book or seeking additional information.

Balducci's
424 Sixth Avenue
New York, NY 10011
mail order

Corti Brothers
5810 Folsom Blvd.
Sacramento, CA 95819
(916) 736-3800
mail order and source for
aceto balsamico tradizionale

Dean & DeLuca
110 Greene Street, Suite 304
New York, NY 10012
mail order and source for
aceto balsamico tradizionale

Foods and Wines from France
24 East 21st Street
New York, NY 10010
(212) 477-9800
information

International Olive Oil Council
P.O. Box 2197, J. A. F. Station
New York, NY 10116
information

International Olive Oil Council
Juan Bravo 10
Madrid 6 Spain
information

NorCal Olive Oil Council
P.O. Box 388
Rutherford, CA 94572
information and assistance
for growers and producers

Olive Oil Hot Line
1-800-232-6548
information

Spectrum Naturals
122 Copeland Street
Petaluma, CA 94952
information

The Vinegar Institute
64 Perimeter Center East
Atlanta, GA 30346
(404) 393-1340
information

INDEX